A V

So
you can cope
with customers?

Video Arts

Cartoons by Shaun Williams

So you think you can cope with customers?

Methuen . Mandarin

A Mandarin Paperback

SO YOU THINK YOU CAN COPE WITH CUSTOMERS?

First published in Great Britain 1989
by Mandarin Books in association with Methuen London
Michelin House, 81 Fulham Road, London SW3 6RB
Mandarin is an imprint of the Octopus Publishing Group.
Copyright © 1989 Video Arts Ltd
Illustrations © 1989 Methuen London

Printed in Great Britain by
Richard Clay Ltd, Bungay, Suffolk

British Library Cataloguing in Publication Data

So you think you can cope with customers?
   Retail trades. Customer relations –
   Manuals
   I. Video Arts
   658.8'7

ISBN 0 7493 0095 7

Contents

Life would be much easier without customers, especially the ones who don't seem to know what they want. Or is it that they don't know what is available? It may be a mixture of the two.

This is one of the fundamental problems of coping with customers. There are two minds at work – yours and the customer's. It is your job to bring them together.

When the slot machine was first installed in 1883, people prophesied that customers wouldn't need sales staff and shops any more. But shops are still around, and good salespeople are in greater demand than ever. Why? Because people need people.

Woman: Which are the cigarettes with the very low tar content?
Tobacconist: Well, the lowest of all are the Mellow Superfine.
Woman: Yes, they're the ones.
Tobacconist: How many?
Woman: Packet of twenty. Can you change this?
Tobacconist: Ten pounds? Yes, of course.
Woman (*looking at her watch*): What time does the chemist open?
Tobacconist: About five to nine.
Woman: Ah, good. Thank you.

An ordinary service, but it would take one hell of a slot machine to provide it. And it's the same with information. Technology allows you to publish more facts than your customers can ever handle – billions of words, every kind of visual display. You can find out all you want to know without ever speaking to a

1 In two minds

Handling customers well

The benefits of handling customers well are two-fold. Firstly, your job becomes more rewarding, as you are developing your techniques while using them and thus feel your job is really worthwhile. Secondly, your customers go away happy, which underlines your pride in becoming more competent. Satisfied customers don't just come back to your firm again, they tend to look for you personally and they also tell their friends to seek you out.

*So you think
you can cope
with customers?*

soul. We ought to be able to abolish people in the service business, but what happens? The good ones are needed more than ever.

For instance, there are plenty of ways to find out facts about trains – computer displays, timetables, pamphlets – but people don't always want to wade through this morass of information.

Customer: What's the best train to Liverpool?
Official: Weekday?
Customer: Yes.
Official: What sort of time?
Customer: Well, after four-thirty.
Official: There's the 1700, that's a fast train.
Customer: Ah. Has it got a restaurant car?
Official: No, but there is a buffet car.
Customer: Ah. Is there a connection to Southport?
Official: Just under twenty minutes' wait.
Customer: Oh good. Can I take the dog?
Official: If you get a ticket for him.
Customer: Oh well. Thanks very much.

Most customers would rather talk to another person, someone who can solve the central problem of customer relations: the problem of two minds – yours and the customer's. When one person approaches another for a product or service, two heads come together, but sometimes the minds inside them fail to meet. Then you have a problem – how to bring those two minds together.

Most people would rather talk to another person.

So you think
you can cope
with customers?

With Horace, you'll never make it.

Customer: Do you do those in any colours except blue?
Horace: Ah. You're about the fiftieth person to ask me that today. No, we don't.
Customer: Why not?
Horace: Well, there's no demand for them.

You can solve the problems of the two minds, as long as you are not a Horace. But you have to realise that there are two sides to it. One side is that the customer doesn't know what is in your mind, what information you could give him about the goods you sell. And the other side is that you don't know what is in the customer's mind about what he wants.

Of course, there are times when it all works perfectly, and there's no problem at all.

Woman: I'm looking for a fridge.
Salesman: Certainly. What height did you want?
Woman: Oh, well, it's got to fit under a thirty-six-inch work surface.
Salesman: Do you want a lot of freezer space?
Woman: No, not necessarily.
Salesman: Do you store a lot of bottles?
Woman: Well, we do get through an awful lot of milk, and some wine and beer.
Salesman: Any particular price range?
Woman: Well, I do want a nice one.
Salesman: I think I know the one you want. It's over here.

Communication

Next time you're in a shop or a bank or post office, look around you at all the confusing information displayed – prices, ingredients, weights, conditions of sale, and so on. It's confusing and, while it may be information, it isn't necessarily communication. Communication is a two-way process, which may differ from customer to customer. Not everyone understands the same meaning from one set of words and you may need a question-and-answer session before you are sure you have perfect understanding. Do realise that there are two sides to the problem. The customer doesn't know what is on your mind – what goods you can offer him. The other side is that you don't know what is on his mind – what he really wants.

Woman: Oh, now that looks just right.

Two things went right. The customer was absolutely clear about what she wanted, and the salesman was absolutely clear about what he'd got. No problems, and so the two minds met.

But it's not always like that. The snag is that when it isn't, it's your job to solve *both* problems. The problem of the customer's mind *and* the problem of *your* mind. That's what it's all about. The problem of your mind is the problem of what's in it. Or in Horace's case, what's not in it.

Customer: Are there direct flights to Frankfurt on Fridays?
Horace: Ah. Frankfurt (*looks frantically but unsuccessfully in book*).
Customer: Yes, Frankfurt.
Horace: Fridays?
Customer: Yes, Fridays.
Horace (*still searching through book*): Well, there should be, shouldn't there?
Customer: Yes, but are there?
Horace: Well, why not? I should think so, yes.
Customer: Look, I don't want guesses. I want to know if there's a direct flight on Friday. Can I depend on it?
Horace: Well, I wouldn't depend on things too much nowadays.
Customer: Or on people!

Ignorance infuriates. So the first rule is this: **know what you've got, know your stock, know the services you give.** That's the bull's-eye, the centre, the heart of the matter.

*So you think
you can cope
with customers?*

Another airline:

Salesman: Ah . . . there's flight BD
126, at 0930 every Friday. Except
Good Friday. That gets in at 1200.
Then there's DH 437 at 2300 –that's
quicker, but it gets in at an awkward
time in the early hours of the
morning.

Customer: No, the first one will do
fine.

But around the basic knowledge of what
you've got and what you haven't, there's
another layer of knowledge: **the rules
your company works by, the conditions customers have to accept.**

Hotel customer: Do you take
cheques?

Horace: Cheques, ah, ah.

Customer: Well, will you accept a
credit card?

Horace: Credit cards? er . . .

Customer: Well, then will you send
the bill on?

Horace (*looking wildly round for help*):
Ah – good question.

Second customer: Can I confirm by
phone or do you have to have a
letter?

Horace: Ah, and another one . . . well
I'll . . .

Second customer: Will you keep
rooms for me until Saturday week?

Horace: Keep them? I'll . . . er . . .
I'll . . .

Customer: Look, what time do you go
off duty?

Horace (*like a flash*): Five-thirty and
not a minute later.

Knowing your
product or service

Many customers need help. You
need to match up the customer's
needs with your knowledge. If you
feel you don't know as much as
you could about your products or
services, ask your manager to
give you some training, or take the
brochures and catalogues home
to study them. Make notes of any
aspects that puzzle you, and keep
asking questions until you are
sure you know all you need to
know.

So, as well as knowing what you've got, you also have to know the rules. But then there's another layer – the one that distinguishes the professionals from the others: **a real knowledge of the business.**

Customer: Are these shoes real leather or plastic?

Horace: Ah . . . yes . . . they could be either, couldn't they?

Browsing girl: It's the new permeable plastic that allows your foot to breathe.

Second customer: Why does this cost more than this?

Horace: Well, it's . . .

Girl: That's real leather and that's a synthetic fabric.

Horace: It's real leather.

Third customer: Are these the ones you advertised in the *Echo*?

Horace: I'm afraid I don't read the *Echo*.

Girl: Yes, they are.

First customer: Are these the same as the ones in the window?

Horace: Ah . . . well, um, what are the ones in the window like?

First customer: Well, they're like these.

Girl: No, the ones in the window have an open toe.

Second customer: Look, it says 'hydrolised'. What does that mean?

Horace: Well, it means that . . . it means that they've been through a hydrolisation process.

Girl: Water resistant.

Horace: And they're water resistant. Yes.

*So you think
you can cope
with customers?*

So the third rule is: **know the business.**
Let's summarise these rules:
First: know what you've got.
Second: know the rules.
Third: know the business.

Well, it says here . . .

There is no substitute for real knowledge.

There's no substitute for real knowledge. If you haven't got it, don't do a Horace and pretend you have.

Customer: Are these pearls real?
Horace: Er . . .
Customer: I mean, they cost enough, don't they?
Horace: Yes, they do.
Customer: So they are real pearls?
Horace: Er . . . yes.
Customer: You're absolutely sure?
Horace: Yes.
Customer: Good. I'll have them.
Horace: Splendid.
Customer: By the way, would you mind writing on the receipt that they are real pearls?
Horace: Write it on the receipt?
Customer: Yes. You see, I'm a lawyer. Handle a lot of prosecutions under the Trade Descriptions Act.
Horace: Prosecutions?
Customer: So I know from experience the great thing is to get it down in writing. Then you can really hammer them.
Horace: Suppose I put 'I think they are real pearls'?
Customer: The law's not interested in what you think.
Horace: Well, I'd . . . uh . . . better get hold of the Manager, then.
Customer (*pointing to Horace's lapel badge*): But you are the Manager.

So there are the three rules for solving one side of the problem – the problem of your mind.

Now for the other side. The problem of the customer's mind. Your problem is

Don't treat people as though they were ghosts by ignoring them.

how to get into it. The door is closed, and the customer is the only one who can open it. This means that encouraging the customer to open that door is the heart of the problem. The customer may be timid, indecisive or unsure of his need. You must find a way of being encouraging without appearing to pester or pressurise, but you must show some sign of interest and encouragement. You don't get people to open doors unless there's a bit of warmth.

Bank assistant: Good morning, sir.
Customer: Good morning. Um, there's something I don't understand on this statement.
Assistant: May I see it? Ah, Mr Wilkinson, is it? Let's see if we can sort it out. Where exactly is the problem?
Customer: Well, it's this cheque I wrote on the 28th – you don't seem to have got it down.
Assistant: No, we don't, do we? Let's have a look. Ah, no, it hasn't been paid in yet. You'll probably get it in next month's statement.
Customer: Ah, that's it, is it? Thank you.

The first rule is: **encourage**. Get the customer to open the door. And the next layer of the target?

Horace: Ah, now that's one of the best cylinder-cut mowers on the market, madam – let me show you, may I?
Customer: No thank you.
Horace: Too large? Well, the small one is tremendous value – it's got a

Don't ignore customers

Don't treat people as though they were ghosts by ignoring them. It creates a chilly atmosphere if you don't acknowledge people because you are too busy chatting or checking your stock. Your stock levels may be important, but customers should always come first. Even if your hands are full of stock, you can still smile and say, 'I won't keep you a minute.'

17

*So you think
you can cope
with customers?*

four-speed gear box.

Customer: No thank you.

Horace: Ah, you're more interested in
the rotary type – well, I can't say I
blame you. Now, this one has the
special double grass-box . . .

Customer: Listen, we live in a flat on
the eighth floor.

Horace: Perhaps the, uh . . . the
carpet's a bit thick, is it?

Customer: We have linoleum.

Horace: Rugs getting shaggy?

Customer: No rugs.

Horace: Well, that's it, isn't it?

Customer: That's it.

The two most valuable aids ever
designed for customer relations are
attached on either side of your head –
your ears. **Listen** for the clues and you
might still make a sale.

Another assistant: Excuse me,
madam, did I hear you say you lived
in a flat?

Customer: That's right.

Assistant: Well, we've just got a new
range of window boxes and indoor
tubs that I thought you might like to
look at . . .

Customer: That's an interesting
thought. (*They go to look at them.*)

Horace: Window box? Well if she
wanted a window box, why didn't
she say so?

If you're going to solve the problem of
the customer's mind, you've got to
explore it – do some **research**. Get the
customer talking, and you will soon find
out what range of goods or services to

offer. If you don't do this, you may find yourself acting like Horace.

Customer: I'd like some advice about a holiday.
Horace: A holiday. Yes. Splendid. Aachen?
Customer: No.
Horace: Abbeville?
Customer: No.
Horace: Addis Ababa?
Customer: No.
Horace: Ajaccio?
Customer: No.
Horace: Alexandria?
Customer: No.
Horace: Algeria?
Customer: No.

Trust Horace to do this the wrong way. 'Yes' and 'No' are the two most unhelpful answers at this stage of research. You have to get the customer to offer something positive.

Another assistant: What sort of holiday were you thinking of, sir?
Customer: Oh, you know, sunbathing, swimming, a bit of golf.
Assistant: Any particular part of the world?
Customer: Oh, I don't know, France or Spain. Or Italy. Not too far.
Assistant: Somewhere quiet, or do you want . . .
Customer: Oh, no, no, no, I like a bit of life. But not too pricey, you know.
Assistant: What about Majorca, say, or Benidorm? Or . . .
Customer: Majorca, yes. I was there a couple of years ago. Sun shining

Open-ended questions

If you ask open-ended questions you invite a descriptive answer. They are called open-ended questions because they can't be answered by 'Yes' or 'No' – the two really unhelpful replies. If you ask, 'Is this what you want?' you will get 'Yes' or 'No' in reply, which leaves you to carry on an interrogation; but if you ask, 'What did you have in mind?' the customer has to give you some detail. So open-ended questions are the ones that start with 'What', 'When', 'Where', 'Who', 'Why' or 'How'.

*So you think
you can cope
with customers?*

all the time. Yes, Majorca. What a good idea.

Meanwhile:

Horace: Zagbia? Zambia? Zanzibar? Zaragossa? Zermatt? . . .

You can sometimes do your research by offering your goods or your services, not as a sales proposal but as more of a market test. Your customer's reactions will give you the pointers to what's in her mind.

Salesgirl: Ah, good morning, madam.
Customer: Oh, good morning. I'm looking for a dress.
Salesgirl: What about this one?
Customer: Bit flighty.
Salesgirl: What about this?
Customer: It's a bit young for me!
Salesgirl: This one, then?
Customer: That one's a bit, well, dowdy.
Salesgirl: What about this one then?
Customer: Bit tweedy.
Salesgirl: I think I know the one.

The problem of your mind

Know what you've got – know your stock, know the services you give.

Know the rules – the rules your company works by, the conditions the customers have to accept.

Know the business.

The problem of the customer's mind

Encourage – get the customer to open the door.

Listen for the clues.

Research – get the customer talking.

Golden rules

2 The meeting of minds

Discover what the customer means

Words mean different things to different people. And even more have a wide range of meaning – such as 'bright', 'large', 'cheap', 'modern', 'convenient'. Be on the lookout for words like these and find out what the customer means by them. Don't assume she means the same as you. That way lies endless confusion and an unhappy customer who thinks you are an idiot, all because you didn't bother to check.

Having realised that there are two minds to be brought together, you need to develop the tool to bring them together. It's called communication. Sometimes it works very well, but all too often something goes wrong. A conversation between two total strangers takes place millions of times every day. One of them is a customer, the other is a member of the sales staff or the service staff.

Customer: Hey, man!
Horace: Good morning, sir.
Customer: Where can I buy something for my doll?
Horace: Toy department, second floor.
Customer: Toy department? She's a bit big for toys.
Horace: Oh, I see. A very large doll?
Customer: Oh, you know. What do the chicks go for?
Horace: Well, about 50 pence each, I think. Pets department, through the arch, second on the right.
Customer: What's in the pets department for my bird?
Horace: Well, lots of things – I mean, cuttlefish, millett, sunflower seeds. A little swing. Does your bird like to swing?
Customer: Oh, she's a swinging chick all right.
Horace: A swinging *chick*? That's most unusual, isn't it?

It's as though there were an invisible barrier between you and the customer. Sometimes you build it yourself. Or at least Horace does.

Customer: I think this is the camera I want. There is just one thing, though . . .

Horace: I know. You're worried about the focus sticking between six and fifteen feet.

Customer: Oh, I didn't realise the focus stuck.

Horace: No, it doesn't, not with this model. So it's the sprocket tearing you're thinking of?

Customer: Does it tear the sprockets?

Horace: No, no, that was the old model. They've put that right now. No, don't even think about it. So it's the delay in the repair shops that's worrying you, is it?

Customer: Do repairs take a long time?

Horace: No, it's much better now. There's hardly any delay – none at all in the winter months.

Customer: I see. Well, perhaps I'd better leave it and think it over.

Horace: What was it that was worrying you?

Customer: I was wondering if it was waterproof?

Horace: Ah, waterproof. No, it's not waterproof.

Customer: I think I must have a waterproof camera.

Trust Horace to build a wall of irrelevant worries and doubts between him and the customer.

You're in danger of building a barrier if you don't see the difference between what you're selling and what the customer is buying. Of course it's the same thing, but it means something very

*So you think
you can cope
with customers?*

Additional sales

The customer who has just bought a pair of shoes may not have the proper polish for them, and won't realise it until he gets home. He may not have the right socks to match the shoes, or shoe trees to keep them in shape. All these are additional sales for you, if you just take the trouble to enquire.

different to each of you. For you, the sale is the end of the business. You're there to serve customers, and you've served them. But for customers, it's only the beginning. This is where they start to use the purchase to satisfy a need.

So look at the problem again. Your mind is full of goods you can offer the customer – all the stocks you carry or can order. Or all the services you can provide – flights, or bookings, or terms of loans or grants or licences. Your skill is in knowing all the alternatives and how they compare.

But the customer's mind is concerned with the use he'll make of the purchase, the end result, the benefit to himself. You see a holiday as a choice of dates, times and prices. He sees himself basking in the sun. You see a dress in terms of fabric, cut, quality and price range. She sees herself making a hit when she arrives at the party. You see a camera in terms of shutter speeds, maximum aperture and focal length. He sees the neighbours admiring the colour slides of his holiday.

Your job is to see the picture in his mind, and let him see into yours. But your technical knowledge can be the barrier that stops you – that stops the meeting of minds.

Like Horace in the bank.

Horace: Well now, what can I do to help you Mrs . . . uh . . .?

Customer: Westbury. I was wondering if you could give me a little more overdraft . . .

Horace: Ah yes. Variable debit facility plan?

Customer: I'm sorry?

Horace: Or were you thinking of the unsecured option repayment loan?

Customer: What?

Horace: Earnings related, or capital related?

Customer: I just want to put an extension on my living-room.

Horace: Ah yes. And you want us to raise your ceiling.

Customer: No, no, the builders will do that. I just want you to lend me the money.

Horace can build a barrier out of anything, but he's really good at it if he can use jargon and technicality.

Don't build a barrier of jargon and technicalities.

*So you think
you can cope
with customers?*

Don't make value judgements

It's a natural reaction to make value judgements about people, such as thinking that because a person is dressed poorly it means he isn't worth serving. But that's not true at all. Rich people often dress casually because they don't feel the need to make an impression. They know they can afford everything in sight and don't have to demonstrate it by the way they dress.

Customer: Have you got a lawnmower that won't be too heavy for me to use?

Horace: Oh yes, madam, this is the perfect machine for you. It's a four-stroke single-cylinder air-cooled engine, helical gear-driven camshaft, mushroom valves, one scraper ring, one compassion ring, flywheel-type magneto ignition, manual control, fully compensating throttle, 75-hour oil-change, low consumption, premium-grade fuel system.

It's no good telling the customer the things *you* want to say. That doesn't remove the barrier. To do that, you have to tell her the things *she* wants to know.

Horace's colleague: The main thing is that it's very safe, very easy to handle and really reliable. No trouble at all.

Customer: Oh well, that sounds exactly what I'm looking for.

So don't build a barrier of jargon and technicalities. Talk to the customer in terms of her end result, the benefit to her.

Before the two minds can meet, there's another part of the barrier to knock down – the customer's own requests, the language he uses.

Wet customer: Do you sell plastic raincoats?

Horace: Ah, no, sir. I'm afraid we don't. Sorry. (*Mutters to himself:*) Honestly, do we look like the kind of shop that sells plastic raincoats? Some people just don't use their brains.

The customer asked for a raincoat, but behind that request was a need to stop getting soaked. It's your job to remove that barrier too.

Customer: Do you sell plastic raincoats?
Horace's assistant: No sir, but we've got quite a good range of umbrellas.
Customer: That'll do just as well. How much are they?

The barrier this customer built was the raincoat. You have to get behind what he thinks he wants, and find what he really needs. What he needed was something to keep the rain off. Let's go back to that waterproof camera.

Customer: I think this is the one I need. There is just one thing, though.
Salesgirl: Yes?
Customer: Is it waterproof?
Salesgirl: No, it's not waterproof. Does that matter?
Customer: I think I need a waterproof camera.
Salesgirl: May I ask exactly why?
Customer: Well, I shall be taking photographs on the beach. All that spray . . .
Salesgirl: Oh, a little bit of spray won't hurt, as long as you wipe the lens.
Customer: Suppose I go out in a boat and a wave comes over?

Why is the customer buying?

Sometimes a customer is inhibited about admitting his or her real motivation. An expert sales assistant can divine this and supply the purchase that satisfies the need, without the real motivation having to be disclosed. Often the indication that there is more to the customer's request than meets the eye is that the items he is asking for seem to be out of character. The simple question 'Is it for you, madam?' will soon tell you if it is to be a gift, or something to help the customer achieve her secret image of herself. A few more carefully worded questions from you should reveal enough to tell you what else is needed to support that image.

*So you think
you can cope
with customers?*

Salesgirl: Ah, well. Then you need our waterproof carrying case. That should take care of accidents like that.

Customer: Um, so you don't think I need an actual waterproof camera?

Salesgirl: Well, you won't actually be photographing while you're swimming, will you?

Customer: No.

Salesgirl: After all, the waterproof version costs three or four times as much.

Customer: Oh, I see. Well, this one with the case will do fine.

The word 'waterproof' was the barrier the customer built. He didn't actually want a waterproof camera at all. The result of the question 'May I ask exactly why?' was that, where Horace had made no sale, this assistant removed the barrier and sold not only the camera but a waterproof case as well.

And quite apart from needing something different from what he asks for, the customer's request may be hiding a lot more than he asks for.

Customer: Got to do some painting. Never tried it before. Could I have a small tin of white paint please?

Horace: Matt or gloss sir?

Customer: Mattaglossa? Is that a good make?

Horace: Shiny or eggshell finish, sir?

Customer: Oh, shiny. Putting up some shelves, you know.

Horace (*handing over tin*): Ah. There you are then. That'll be £2.65 please.

Customer (*handing over money*): Oh, fine. Thanks very much. (*And he walks off.*)

Horace: Wonder why he didn't buy any undercoat? Probably never thought of it.

This time the barrier was the tin of paint. Let's see what was behind it.

Customer: Got to do some painting. Never tried it before. Could I have a small tin of white paint please?

Salesgirl: Shiny finish or dull finish?

Customer: Oh, shiny, putting up some shelves, you know.

Salesgirl: Undercoat and primer?

Customer: Oh yes, I suppose I'll want those too.

Salesgirl: Sandpaper to rub down with?

Customer: Do you have to do that? Yes.

Salesgirl: Brushes?

Customer: Yes.

Salesgirl: And a cleaner to clean them with?

Customer: Good idea.

Salesgirl: Now what about the shelving?

Customer: Well, I'm going to have a bash at doing it myself.

Salesgirl: But have you got a carpentry saw?

Customer: Come to think of it I haven't.

Salesgirl: What about a drill for the screws?

Customer: Good thinking.

Salesgirl: And a set of bits for the drill? Screws, rawlplugs?

Stress the benefits

Talk to the customer in terms of what she will get. Customers want to know what products or services will do for them – this is what persuades them to buy. It's known as 'selling the sizzle, not just the sausage'. Stressing the benefits of the purchase reassures the customer that she has made the right decision in buying this item.

*So you think
you can cope
with customers?*

Customer: My goodness, you know a
lot about it. Hey, you're not free on
Sunday morning, are you?

This time the request barrier was hiding
a complicated need, and the assistant
understood it much better than the
customer. He wouldn't have started on
his shelves until Sunday – and would
have found all the things he was missing
only when it was too late.

The masters of customer relations
become experts in something more than
the goods they sell or the service they
offer. They become experts in human
nature.

Customer: Just wondered if you had a
floral tie?
Salesman: What will you be wearing
it with, sir?
Customer: Well, you know . . .

You may need to be a bit of a psychiatrist to look for the reason behind the
request.

Psychiatrist: Floral tie? Why do you
want to wear a floral tie? Do you
feel it will make you look younger?
Customer: My wife says I'm getting
stuck in the mud.
Psychiatrist: Tell me about it.
Customer: It's not only my wife, it's
the children too. They say I'm
fuddy-duddy. Out of date. Out of
touch. And the secretaries at work –
I feel they giggle at me, I'm
becoming a sort of joke.
Psychiatrist: But you don't feel like
that inside?

'Identity' purchases

'Identity' purchases are those
where the customer is influenced
by the opinion other people will
form of him or her because of that
purchase. Clothing is an obvious
example, but there are many
others, like the place we choose
for a holiday or the car we drive.
It's that secret image again, and
all you need to do to make these
customers happy is to treat them
as though you see them as the
sort of person they want to be.

Customer: No. I feel quite jolly –
quite mischievous. I used to be a bit
of a lad. And then, when I see
myself in the mirror, it doesn't seem
to fit.

If you know what's in the customer's
mind when he makes his request, you
stand a better chance of selling him
what he really wants.

Customer (*in new outfit*): Marvellous.
Oh, I do like that. I can't wait to get
home. Can't wait to see my
Cynthia's face. Marvellous. Thank
you. Thank you very much.
Salesman: It's a pleasure, sir.

So let's summarise the techniques for
bringing about a meeting of minds. First
you get inside the customer's mind and
find the picture inside. Then you present
what he wants in terms of the benefit to
him.

You explain the goods in simple terms
that the customer can understand, with
no trade jargon or baffling technicality.

Finally, you remember that the customer may need something different
from what she asks for. That way you
remove the barriers and achieve the
meeting of minds.

Remember, where there's no understanding, there's no sale.

Enter into the spirit

To you the sale is the end of the
business. To the customer it's only
the beginning. You see a diamond
ring as an object, something to
sell. He sees it as something
romantic and exciting – a special
present for a special person. Don't
spoil his fun by being matter-of-
fact about this sort of purchase –
enter into the spirit of things and it
will brighten the day for both of
you – and bring that customer
back next time he wants a special
present for someone he loves.

*So you think
you can cope
with customers?*

You don't *have* to pump iron
to keep fit – there are other ways . . .

Remember that the customer may need
something different from what she asks for.

To get inside the customer's mind and find the picture inside:

> Listen.
> Encourage.
> Explore.

To make sure the customer understands you:

> Use simple terms.
> Be positive.
> Describe products and services in terms of benefits.

Golden rules

3 Awkward customers

Defuse the customer's anger

When people are rude or angry, our first reaction is to think it is because of something we ourselves have done wrong. We become defensive, even emotional, and therefore we handle the situation badly. Once you realise that you are receiving the brunt of the customer's anger for no other reason than the fact that you are handy and a captive audience, it helps you to see the encounter not as a personal conflict but as a professional challenge. You can then stand back and let it all wash over you while you listen for the key words that will let you defuse the customer's anger and put things right.

Every customer needs slightly different treatment. Most of them aren't too much of a problem, but some can be difficult, really awkward. If you can handle them, you're a real professional. Anyone can get on with the easy types, but you need to be good at your job to deal with the angry, the downright rude or the featherbrained.

You'll recognise Mr Tiger. He's angry. He's been waiting about for nearly ten minutes, or somebody's given him the wrong information, or he's got flu coming on, or his wife just crashed the car. It doesn't matter which, he's angry and he's going to vent his anger on someone, and he isn't prepared to stop being angry just like that.

Let's see how Brian copes with him.

Mr Tiger: What's going on here? Ten minutes I've been waiting at this window and nobody's been near me.

Brian: Look, I've been back there getting information for another customer.

Mr Tiger: Well, somebody else should attend to that.

Brian: That's not my fault, is it? I don't run the place.

Mr Tiger: Ten minutes I've been here and I'm in a hurry.

Brian: Well, you've got to wait your turn, haven't you?

Mr Tiger: What?

Brian: You can't just swan in here and get served just like that. I mean, we're busy.

Mr Tiger: Swan in? I might tell you I've been a customer of this bank for thirty years!

Brian: Come on, come on, what do you want? There are people waiting.

Mr Tiger: How dare you speak to me like that!

Brian: Just because you've got a fancy tie doesn't make you more important than the others. Now, what do you *want*?

Mr Tiger: I want to see the Manager. I refuse to put up with this impertinence. (*He proceeds to have a mild cardiac arrest.*)

That approach doesn't work. The bank now has one very angry customer, because Brian couldn't handle him, because he didn't react like a professional. Instead of staying cool, he allowed himself to get personally involved, so he was rude – and rudeness never works. So rule one is: **don't get personally involved – keep a professional distance.**

Let's give Brenda a chance to see what she can do.

Mr Tiger: They sent me here from your other office, and when I get here it's ten minutes before anyone condescends to serve me.

Brenda: I'm sorry but we're very busy at the moment, sir.

Mr Tiger: I don't care about that. Why did it take me ten minutes to get served?

Brenda: Because there are a lot of customers in here, sir.

Mr Tiger: Well, why aren't there more assistants?

Brenda: Well, we have to stagger our lunch hour, sir. We can't all go at the same time.

Don't get angry

If a customer is angry, never let yourself get angry back. It can only turn an unpleasant little incident into an unpleasant big incident. If you realise that there is a good reason for that anger you are in a better position to locate the reason and correct it than if you take the stance that the only thing wrong is the customer's manners. In an ideal world, customers would behave towards you as they do to their friends. But this is not an ideal world, and many customers are convinced that their decision to spend their money with your company entitles them to leave their manners at home. Don't let it worry you – just get on with helping them to spend their money.

Don't get involved – keep a professional distance.

Mr Tiger: I'm not suggesting you all go at the same time. What I *am* suggesting is that there are more of you here when you're busy so that people don't have to hang about for ten minutes before they get served.

Brenda: It's not usually so busy at this time, sir. If we knew when it was going to be busy, we could plan accordingly.

Mr Tiger: I often come in here at this time and I would say that it was a very busy time indeed.

Brenda: It is a fairly busy time normally, sir, but it's not usually as busy as *this*.

They've now been at it for a minute and a half. Brenda's not been rude and she's not let Mr Tiger walk all over her. Good for her – but the customer is just as angry as he was when they started, so she's actually got nowhere. The whole point about Mr Tiger is that you don't get anywhere until you've calmed him down. So calm him down as quickly as possible; then you can get on with it.

Maybe Brian can calm him down.

Mr Tiger: It took me a quarter of an hour to find this place because everyone in your wretched store misdirected me.

Brian: Oh, I'm sorry to hear that, sir.

Mr Tiger: I thought you were all supposed to know where every department is?

Brian: We are, sir, yes, we certainly are.

Mr Tiger: I asked three different assistants.

*So you think
you can cope
with customers?*

Brian: I am sorry, sir, that really is
bad.

Mr Tiger: Bad? It's appalling!

Brian: I can't apologise too much.

Mr Tiger: And when I do get here, it
takes me ten minutes to get served.

Brian: I'm very sorry, sir, but we're
very understaffed at the moment.

Mr Tiger: W—well, anyway, yesterday
that man sold me this and it is the
wrong size.

Brian: I'm so sorry, but I'm afraid he
is new here.

Mr Tiger: Not only the wrong size but
there's a button missing.

Brian: Oh, not again! I've told him
about that sort of thing. They really
should have checked.

Mr Tiger: Yes, they should.

Brian: Please accept my apologies, sir.

Mr Tiger: Well, anyway, you seem to
know what you're doing.

Brian: Oh thank you very much, sir.
Now, may I change this for you?

Mr Tiger: No thank you. Money back.

Brian: You wouldn't be interested in
any of these?

Mr Tiger: No, I don't think I'll risk
anything else in this store. (*He
laughs.*)

Brian: Actually, these aren't too bad.

Mr Tiger: No thank you. Refund
please.

Brian eventually calmed Mr Tiger
down, but at the cost of destroying his
confidence in Brian's firm. Wherever
you work, mistakes are going to be
made. Your job is to sort them out, not
to draw attention to them by apologising
at length for them. The way to deal with

the angry customer is just to apologise for the *specific* inconvenience he's suffered, no more, and then *straight* away to start putting it right.

Let's give Brenda another try. Mr Tiger is at a hotel reception desk, fuming. Brenda finishes with another customer to deal with Mr Tiger.

Brenda: Good evening, sir.

Mr Tiger: Ten minutes I've been waiting here for someone to attend to me.

Brenda: I'm very sorry we've kept you waiting, sir, can I help . . .

Mr Tiger: Ten minutes!

Brenda: Well, we won't waste your time any longer, sir.

Mr Tiger: I should hope not. I'm already late for a meeting, that telephone's out of order and your porter has disappeared with my luggage.

Brenda: Have you got an urgent call to make, sir?

Mr Tiger: They're waiting for me now.

Brenda: I'll get a call on this line, sir (*picking up the phone on her desk*). Have you got the number?

Mr Tiger hands a card to Brenda and she asks the switchboard to get the number.

Brenda: Would you like a taxi, sir?

Mr Tiger: No, I have a car. Why are you the only one here?

Brenda: Because another guest wanted something done in a hurry, sir. Would you like to check in, sir?

Mr Tiger: No, I haven't the time now.

Don't grovel

You will not help an angry customer to calm down by grovelling. This not only implies that you accept his assumption that the company is generally inefficient, but serves to convince him that the malaise is widespread. It is far better to apologise briefly and state with conviction that his unhappy experience has been an exception to the general rule of competence.

Oh how dreadful, sir – would you like to make an appointment to see one of our apologisers?

The way to deal with the angry customer is just to apologise for the specific inconvenience he suffered, no more, then straight away to start putting it right.

God knows what's happened to my luggage.

Brenda: Oh. I'll track it down and have it put in your room, sir. Would you like a single room?

Mr Tiger: Yes. Do your porters usually walk off with other people's property?

Brenda: No, sir. But we're very glad you've told us, sir, it certainly won't happen again. Would you like a room with a bath, sir?

Mr Tiger: Yes.

Brenda: Ah, here's your call.

Mr Tiger (*into telephone*): Hello, George Tiger here. Will you please tell Mr Benson that I shall be about twenty minutes late and that I'm sorry.

Brenda (*handing him a registration card*): Just your name and address, sir, if you don't mind. I'll fill in the rest later. Your room number is 321 and I'll have your luggage put in there, sir. Do you know the way, sir, or would you like this map?

Mr Tiger: Oh. Thank you.

Brenda: So sorry to have kept you waiting, sir.

That's the right way to deal with Mr Tiger. Not by arguing or excessively apologising, but by getting on with what has to be done.

Sure, he's going to let off some steam, but getting things done cools Mr Tiger off faster than anything. So, rule one is: **keep a professional distance and don't get involved.** Rule two is: **apologise for the specific cause of his anger and start doing something about it.**

*So you think
you can cope
with customers?*

Don't judge the goods

Do not fuel a rude customer's abuse by making value judgements about the goods he is inspecting. Telling him that something is 'good value' or 'the best' or 'attractive' merely gives him the opportunity for further rudeness about your personal taste and experience. It is far better to stick to factual descriptions like '100 per cent wool' or 'Italian design'. Remember that the offensive customer is offensive to everyone. Your job isn't to make him nice, but simply to supply him with what he came for.

That's Mr Tiger, then. Not very nice to start with, but OK when you calm him down. Unlike Mr Warthog, who is a very ugly customer indeed. Here he is, looking at radios.

Mr Warthog: Bloody rubbish!

Brian: That one's very good value, sir.

Mr Warthog: Who are you kidding? None of these give you proper reception, you know. I mean, look at the finish on that one.

Brian: Well, that's the least expensive model we have, sir.

Mr Warthog: Cheap, is it?

Brian: Well . . . no, not, not . . .

Mr Warthog: It looks it. It's garbage. It's all garbage.

Brian: This is a better model, sir.

Mr Warthog: Look, the selector button on that doesn't work properly.

Brian: I think it does.

Mr Warthog: My son-in-law's got one and I'm telling you that it doesn't.

Brian: Well, it's perfectly easy to get it put right. I mean . . .

Mr Warthog: £35.50 for that?

Brian: Oh well, it's a lovely job, sir.

Mr Warthog: No it isn't. I mean, look at that Japanese muck.

Brian: Well, it's . . . it's very well thought of.

Mr Warthog: Not where I stand, it isn't. It is very badly thought of right here. I wouldn't give you the time of day for it. It's garbage.

Brian: The . . . the . . . this is a beauty, sir.

Mr Warthog: No it isn't.

Brian: It is, really.

Mr Warthog: No it is not.

Brian (*who is now getting upset*): It is! I
  promise.
Mr Warthog: It is not. It's garbage.
  All you get on it is interference.
Brian: You don't get interference on it.
Mr Warthog: Yes you do.

*Brian bursts into tears and Mr
Warthog laughs at him.*

Mr Warthog is rude. Not angry like Mr
Tiger, just plain old-fashioned rude.
And you can't stop it. He's going to be
unpleasant the whole time and you've
got to handle him *while* he's being
unpleasant.
  Maybe Brenda can do better with
him.

Mr Warthog: I want to see Mr
  Billington.
Brenda: Oh, I'm afraid Mr Billington
  isn't here at the moment, sir.
Mr Warthog: He never is, is he?
Brenda: Well, I don't think . . .
Mr Warthog: When's he back?
Brenda: I don't know exactly when
  he'll be back, sir. Have you an
  appointment?
Mr Warthog: No I don't.
Brenda: Well, then, you can hardly be
  surprised that he's . . .
Mr Warthog: Look, I do a lot of
  business with this firm, right? And
  this is important. Now then, when's
  he back?
Brenda (*deliberately casual*): If you'd
  like to sit down over there, sir,
  I'll try and find out when he's due
  back and if he can see you
  today.

Mr Warthog: Today! Now look here . . .

Brenda: You can hardly be surprised, sir. If Mr Billington isn't here, then you won't be able to see him.

Mr Warthog: I don't get this sort of bureaucratic nonsense at Timpson's.

Brenda: Oh, don't you?

Mr Warthog: No I don't. If I want to see someone there, I just walk in.

Brenda: Even if they're not there?

Mr Warthog: Well, if they're not there someone else sees me. They know where their staff are.

Brenda: Oh, well, perhaps it would be better if you dealt with them, sir.

Mr Warthog: Aye, perhaps it would.
(*He stomps out.*)

It's not difficult to let Mr Warthog rile you, but you mustn't. You've got to stay cool. And one thing may help you to do this. The key to Mr Warthog is that deep down, underneath all that rudeness, he is in fact very unpleasant. To everyone, without fear or favour. When he's dealing with the people up the road, he's telling them how bad they are and how much better your firm is. So don't take it personally. Stay cool, ignore the rudeness and get on with it.

Let's try that again.

Mr Warthog: Billington!

Brenda: Good morning, sir.

Mr Warthog: Billington!

Brenda: I'm sorry?

Mr Warthog: I want to see Mr Billington.

Brenda: I'm afraid Mr Billington isn't here at the moment, sir.

Mr Warthog: He never is, is he?

Brenda: Do you have an appointment?

Mr Warthog: No I don't. Where the hell is he?

Brenda: I'll try and find out. May I have your name please?

Mr Warthog: Warthog. They don't keep me hanging around like this at Timpson's you know. They know where their staff are!

Brenda (*into telephone*): Hello Audrey, could you tell me when Mr Billington will be able to see Mr Warthog please . . . four o'clock?

Mr Warthog: Oh Christ.

Brenda (*into telephone*): Hang on, Audrey. (*To Mr Warthog:*) Can you tell me what you want to see Mr Billington about, sir?

Mr Warthog: About the exhibition stand.

Brenda: Audrey, do you know anyone who can help us with an exhibition stand? Oh, thank you. Mr Warthog, Mr Alexander should be able to help you with that, but he's got someone with him at the moment. He'll be able to see you in ten minutes. Do you mind waiting?

Mr Warthog: Yes, I do.

Brenda: Would you prefer me to make you an appointment with Mr Billington?

Mr Warthog: No, I'll wait.

Remember, Mr Warthog is like that to everyone. Try to ignore the rudeness and get on with it. Don't take it personally, just turn him into a customer and then you're a real professional.

Mr Warthog is the same to everybody.

Even without being angry or rude, however, customers can still be awkward. Take Mrs Rabbit, for instance. She's much nicer, but just as much trouble in her own way. Here she is, trying to buy a bottle of shoecleaner.

Brian: Good morning, madam. Are you being attended to?

Mrs Rabbit: Well, no, I want something to clean my shoes with, you see. I got salt water on them when I was in Spain, you see – we went down on the beach with our grandchildren, you know, just to keep an eye on them, mind you the eldest is six now, quite a big girl . . .

Brian: I see, yes, well about colour . . .

Mrs Rabbit: She was right out in the water, up to here, one minute she was paddling about in front of us, and the next, there she was, right out in the water, up to her neck . . .

Brian: Up to her neck – well, now, what about colour?

Mrs Rabbit: Yes, miles out, she was, miles out. 'Cos she's tall for her age, like her father, you know. Of course, he's not quite as tall as you, he's broad, you know.

Brian: Well . . .

Mrs Rabbit: Anyway, she's tall and she was right out there in the water, up to her neck. Of course we didn't know where she'd gone. Well, we were scared out of our wits. Well, you are, aren't you?

Brian: Yes, yes, you are, yes.

Mrs Rabbit: Yes!

Brian: Well, what colour are . . .

Mrs Rabbit: We started running up

Don't show boredom

The challenge with a chattering customer is not to show that you are bored or frustrated by your inability to shut her up. Take a tip from television interviewers. They use conversational gaps in a very clever way, not by interrupting with a long preamble, but by getting straight to the point. Avoid 'Now can we get back to discussing your car engine?' and use 'The engine is knocking. Yes?'

47

*So you think
you can cope
with customers?*

and down the beach like mad things.
What the other people on the beach
must have thought, I do not know.
And there she was, all the time, out
in the water and we were running
up and down the beach looking for
her.

It may be tempting to cut this off
abruptly, but you must never show
annoyance with Mrs Rabbit. It's rude,
and that never works. Nor must you
show you're bored. That's rude too, and
it still doesn't stop her chatting on and
on. You can't stop Mrs Rabbit talking.
She's a compulsive talker. All you can
do is to lead her so that she talks about
what you want her to talk about. Try
again, Brian.

Brian: Good morning, madam.
Mrs Rabbit: Oh, good morning. I
want something to clean my shoes
with, you see. I got salt water on
them when I was in Spain, you see –
we went down on the beach with our
grandchildren, you know . . .
Brian: Ah, and the sea got on them,
did it?
Mrs Rabbit: Well, yes, because we
had to go in after one of them, she
wandered out a bit too far, you see.
Brian: And they're stained, are they?
Mrs Rabbit: And well, yes, 'cos she's
only six so we had to go in and get
her out, you see, we never thought
she'd go in as far as that and . . .
Brian: Of course not. Did she have
shoes on?
Mrs Rabbit: And, uh, no, she had
bare feet actually.

Brian: But you had to go in with yours on.

Mrs Rabbit: Well, yes, you see, we had to go in and get her out, you see, she went out ever so far. She was up to here in the water.

Brian: Oh dear. Are they leather or suede?

Mrs Rabbit: She was miles out, she was. Up to her neck in the water.

Brian: Are they leather or suede?

Mrs Rabbit: Oh, they're leather.

Brian: Leather, yes.

Mrs Rabbit: I got them to go with this dress. 'Cos we knew it was going to be warm in Spain you see.

Brian: What colour dress?

Mrs Rabbit: Well, it's a sort of beigy-brown really, light, summery, feathery sort of . . .

Brian: I see, and the shoes are light brown too, are they?

Mrs Rabbit: Well, yes, they are to go with the dress, you see . . . because I always think you really do want to have a good appearance.

Brian: Of course you do. Well, I think I've got the thing for you.

Mrs Rabbit: Eh? Of course, I mean you never know when you might be going up for tea, do you? Off the beach? You want to look . . .

Brian: Absolutely! Do you want the big one or the small one?

Mrs Rabbit: Oh, that looks like the very thing.

Supply catalogues or brochures

It is useful to have a stock of devices to shut up the rabbiters, and to keep them occupied for a while so you can break away and serve other customers. A stock of catalogues or brochures for them to look at are wonderful devices to use for this purpose. Hand them over a few at a time, and it gives the impression that you have their needs in mind even when you are serving someone else.

That's the way to deal with Mrs Rabbit. Whenever she gets off the point, lead her back on, again and again. She's a compulsive talker and a time-waster if

*So you think
you can cope
with customers?*

you don't handle her firmly. Firmly but politely. Don't show boredom or irritation, don't interrupt or talk her down, just stay cool and keep leading her back to the point.

My husband refuses to go on holiday while the delphiniums are in bloom, so this means . . . witter, witter, witter . . .

Don't show boredom.

With angry customers
Don't waste time by arguing, apologise
for the specific inconvenience and no
more, and get on with what they want.

With rude customers
Ignore the rudeness and deal with
them as you would any other customer.

With chatterboxes
Don't show your irritation or boredom,
just keep leading them back to the
point.

With all of them
Stay cool.
Don't get personally involved.
Keep a professional distance.

Golden rules

4 More awkward customers

Don't let customers under your skin

The ability to handle members of the awkward squad obviously increases with experience. You will become more alert and sensitive to individual customer types and learn how to handle them. The first rule in handling them is not to let their awkwardness get under your skin.

Unfortunately, Mr Tiger, Mr Warthog and Mrs Rabbit aren't the only awkward customers you will meet. There are also the ones who want to prove their superiority, the ones who are deeply suspicious of everything, and the ones who just hate to talk. Just like the others, you deal with them by using your knowledge – knowledge *of* what you sell, knowledge *about* what you sell, and knowledge *of* your company's rules.

You'll know Mrs Camel's type – haughty, snotty, determined to show how grand she is, and if she can put you down that makes her feel even grander. So, if you don't know your stuff, she'll be delighted.

Mrs Camel: *Formaggio della campagna.*
Brian: I beg your pardon?
Mrs Camel: *Formaggio della campagna*, please. It's cheese.
Brian: Ah, what was it called again?
Mrs Camel: *Formaggio della campagna.* Would you like me to write it down?
Brian: Oh no, well, we've got Camembert, Brie, Port Salut . . .
Mrs Camel: Oh dear.
Brian: Sorry?
Mrs Camel: It's Italian, not French. You've heard of Italy, have you?
Brian: Er, yes.
Mrs Camel: Well, it's not France you see – totally different neighbourhood.
Brian: Well, we've got Gorgonzola, Pipa di Crema, er . . .
Mrs Camel: Oh dear!
Brian: Er . . . Limburger.
Mrs Camel: That is German. You do belong on this counter, do you?

Brian: Yes!

Mrs Camel: I mean you haven't just got in there by mistake, have you? Because I'm sure we could have you rescued if you have . . .

Brian: No, no, no.

Mrs Camel: Oh, they actually pay you to work around here, do they?

Brian: Yes.

Mrs Camel: How quaint. But, aren't you really supposed to know what to sell?

If Mrs Camel can make you feel like the scum of the earth, she will. Of course, there's one easy way to stop her putting you through that sort of humiliation.

Mrs Camel: Do you have Jasek's recording of Prokofiev's Opus No. 63 with the PSO?

Brian: Ah. No.

Mrs Camel: Heiferz with Munch and LA Phil?

Brian: No. No.

Mrs Camel: I see! Opus 55 then, the No. 5 in G Minor, Richter and the WSO with Rowicki?

Brian: No.

This is the old 'No' routine. Magic really – you keep saying no and eventually the customer disappears. It's quite painless – but you don't sell anything.

There's no magic way out with Mrs Camel. You've simply got to build up a really good knowledge of the business, but even when you have acquired that there is still a wrong way of handling her.

*So you think
you can cope
with customers?*

Mrs Camel: Waiter! Cheese! *Formaggio della campagna.*

Brian: From which region, madam?

Mrs Camel: I beg your pardon?

Brian: *Formaggio della campagna* merely means cheese of the region. To which region are you particularly referring?

Mrs Camel: Well, that's what it's called.

Brian: Ah . . . I'm not making myself clear, I'm afraid. There are many cheeses called *formaggio della campagna.* I don't known what cheese you want, until you tell me to which region you are referring.

Mrs Camel: Well, we ate it when we were on holiday.

Brian: In which region, madam?

Mrs Camel: We were staying at Pietrasanta.

Brian: Ah, now is that Tuscany or Liguria?

Mrs Camel: Well, I er . . .

Brian: Or Emilio Romagna perhaps. You see, there are over forty local cheeses in Liguria alone, so it's rather difficult to guess which one you're after. Was it firmer than a Bel Paese?

Mrs Camel: Er, firmer than a what?

Brian: Or a Savoyard?

Mrs Camel: Savoyard?

Brian: Was it full-fat or semi-curd?

Mrs Camel: Full fat, er, I . . .

Brian: Was it a goat's milk cheese, perhaps? Or a variety of *scoppolini*?

Mrs Camel: *Scoppolini*?

Brian: It is cheese, is it? You know, cheese – the stuff they make from milk?

It's a temptation to get your own back on someone as snotty as Mrs Camel, but if you are going to sell her anything it's a temptation you've got to resist. You've got to stop her walking all over you, but you've got to use your expertise not to put her down, but to raise yourself up to her level. Not above it, to it.

Mrs Camel: *Formaggio della campagna.*
Brian: From which region, madam?
Mrs Camel: I beg your pardon?
Brian: Well, they vary a lot from region to region. Was there a particular type?
Mrs Camel: We ate it when we were on holiday at Pietrasanta.
Brian: I see, was it firmer than a Bel Paese?
Mrs Camel: A what?
Brian: Firmer than this one?
Mrs Camel: No, it's much softer than that.

That was all right, but Brian did miss one little trick. The difference between dealing with Mrs Camel well and really well is a simple little trick that works on all customers, but it works best of all on Mrs Camel – flattery. We all like a bit of flattery, but Mrs Camel dotes on it. After all, she wants to impress people, so if you can treat her as though her knowledge and taste are a bit special, you'll have her eating out of your hand.

Try saying 'As you know, madam' when telling her something she may not know, or 'Not many people understand that, madam' when she displays a bit of expertise. Avoid telling her the obvious, which shows you think she's ignorant.

Never embarrass a customer

Mrs Camel is a show-off at heart and any form of praise will reinforce her high opinion of herself. With praise and compliments you will be able to lead her to many buying decisions which she will then think she has made on her own. Part of her routine is to pose as an expert or connoisseur, so be careful not to squash her by showing you know how little she really knows. You may win an argument, but you will lose a customer if you embarrass her.

We don't have anything like *that*, but if madam has a few petrol coupons she could try her local garage.

It's a temptation to get your own back on someone as snotty as Mrs Camel.

And, if she gets something hopelessly wrong, 'Ah, now that's a mistake I'm always making myself' avoids having to put her down.

Brenda: Hello? Enquiries.

Mrs Camel: I wish to make a complaint about my post this morning.

Brenda: Would you give me the details, madam. I hope I can help you.

Mrs Camel: When it arrived, the postman asked my son to pay postage on three letters and a parcel that had been forwarded to us.

Brenda: I see.

Mrs Camel: And I've just checked and the postage was absolutely correct.

Brenda: Ah, that's very helpful, madam.

Mrs Camel: So I fail to see why I've been charged.

Brenda: Well, some of the regulations are a little involved. Did you arrange with your old post office to forward mail to you?

Mrs Camel: That's not necessary, is it?

Brenda: No, quite right, it isn't necessary.

Mrs Camel: The new owners said they'd send everything on – the letters hadn't been opened.

Brenda: Ah, you obviously understand about this, madam, but may I ask, had they been forwarded later than the day after they were received?

Mrs Camel: Er, oh yes, but there's nothing about that in your pamphlet.

Flattery works wonders

Show-offs want to impress you and nothing pleases them like evidence that they have succeeded. If you supply that evidence, you will find them very easy to deal with. Flattery always works wonders and the best way to apply it is by imparting information with the useful phrase 'As you know . . .'

So you think
you can cope
with customers?

Brenda: Is that the Redirection of Mail pamphlet?

Mrs Camel: Yes.

Brenda: Oh, I wish more people had the right pamphlet to hand. Thank you, madam. Well, if you look on the front, I'm not surprised you missed it. It's rather hidden under the bit about Private Redirection.

Mrs Camel: Oh, but now . . . what about that parcel? That wasn't delayed – that was posted immediately.

Brenda: I'm afraid that with redirected parcels, the original postage is payable again.

Mrs Camel: Are you perfectly sure?

Brenda: It's on the back under Redirection of Parcels.

Mrs Camel: Ah, well, I wasn't to know that.

Brenda: Well, you're in very good company, madam. Very few people do. It's perfectly natural to assume the rules are the same for all mail. Does that answer your query?

Mrs Camel: Yes, yes, it does.

Brenda: Thank you for checking with us, madam. It helps us avoid mistakes. Of course, if you did arrange with your old post office to forward your mail, it would save delay in redirection.

That is, of course, the way to do it with Mrs Camel. She'll walk all over you if you don't know your stuff. So rule one is: **make sure you do know your stuff.** Rule two is: **don't put her down; if anything, build her up a bit – flatter her knowledge or taste.** It works with everyone, but best of all with her.

Mr Clam is quite different. He's so quiet you wonder if he's had his tongue amputated, or joined a monastery and taken a vow of silence. It's not rudeness – he just doesn't like to talk. He doesn't much like listening, either. Especially to sales chat. Basically, Mr Clam just wants to be left alone.

Brian: Can I help you, sir?
Mr Clam: No, thanks.
Brian: Fine . . . right . . . well, I'll not help you then. Right, well look, I'll just go away, if that's all right by you? I'll be over there if you want to keep away from me.
Mr Clam: Thanks.
Brian: No, not at all. Glad to have not been of help.

Wrong. 'Can I help you' is a bad opening remark because if you get the answer 'No' you can't try again without seeming pushy. This is a bad policy with any customer, not just with Mr Clam, but no good salesman ever leaves a customer completely alone.

Sometimes, when your merchandise is clearly displayed with the relevant information clearly marked, and the range of your stock and its comparative merits are pretty obvious, it may be all right to let customers look for themselves. But usually that's not good enough – usually the salesperson has got to find out what is in the customer's mind, and that means getting him to talk.

It may be difficult, but you must give it a try. Start by giving him a brief piece of factual information. This is where

*So you think
you can cope
with customers?*

Resist the temptation to chatter

It is very difficult to wait out a long silence, so with a customer like Mr Clam, who acts as though he has had his tongue amputated, you will be tempted to gibber, say anything, to fill that awful silence. But that is just what he hates most, so be patient and resist the temptation to chatter. Once he realises you are not going to pester him or pressurise him, he may open up a little and give you some information on what he wants. Keep your questions open-ended, or he'll retire back behind his wall of silence with a one-word answer – usually 'No'!

your knowledge of your merchandise is absolutely vital. It gives you an enormous range of opening remarks.

Like here, when Mr Clam has just picked up an electric carving knife.

Brian: That one works off the mains, sir, but there's a battery-operated one, if you prefer it.

If he reacts unfavourably, just move off and try again later. Not immediately, because Mr Clam doesn't like being hustled. Give him a couple of minutes.

Brian: The blade is stainless steel, sir. And the handle is heat resistant.

That's the way, but you mustn't hustle him. Take your time but keep trying.

Brian: That one's lighter than the other, sir, so it might be easier for a woman to operate.
Mr Clam: Yes, that's true.
Brian: You don't have to exert any pressure or make any sawing movements. You know, just guide, so it's rather good for cutting delicate things like sponges or fruit cake.
Mr Clam: Ha ha, sponges.

Once you've got him interested, you can ask him a question.

Brian: You prefer the mains-operated one to the battery-operated one, do you, sir?
Mr Clam: I do really, yes.

Use brief factual comments until you feel you've established contact, then start to find out what's in his mind.

Brenda: Good morning, Mr Clam. Not your usual weekly amount? Are you sure you need all this in cash? I mean, could you use a cheque?

Mr Clam: I'm going abroad.

Brenda: Oh, abroad? Won't you need travellers' cheques?

Mr Clam: I'm going to buy them.

Brenda: I can arrange them for you now if you like.

Mr Clam: Oh. All right.

So you sell to Mr Clam by making short factual remarks until you've established contact, then you can find out what he needs.

Meanwhile, back at the electrical counter, he's looking at blenders. Brenda has had two attempts so far. She tried, 'The larger one has some extra safety features,' and, 'It's got a screw-on cap, so there is no danger of spilling when you switch it on . . . this one has a larger bowl, sir, and more attachments.'

Mr Clam: Too expensive.

Brenda: Do you need all the attachments, sir?

Mr Clam: No.

Brenda: Well, do you need it for anything in particular?

Mr Clam: Coffee.

Brenda: Grinding coffee?

Mr Clam: Ummmmm . . .

Brenda: Oh well, if that's all you need it for, what about this simple coffee-

61

So you think
you can cope
with customers?

grinder? It's about a fifth of the cost. Do you need it for anything else?

Mr Clam: No.

That's Mr Clam. He doesn't like talking or being talked at, either. So, rule one is: **don't chatter at him and don't say, 'Can I help you?' – use short factual remarks to establish contact.** Rule two is: **if at first you don't succeed, move away and try again later.**

Remember, when you're dealing with any customer you've got to find out as much as you can about what is in their minds. The short factual comments you use on Mr Clam will help you to do this with all sorts of customers. And the only way you can come up with these opening remarks is to have a really first-class knowledge of the goods you're dealing with.

That expert knowledge is equally important when you have to deal with Mrs Ferret, the suspicious one. She'll soon find out if you know your stuff.

Mrs Ferret: Well, you did say this was washable, didn't you?

Brenda: Oh yes, madam.

Mrs Ferret: You're absolutely sure?

Brenda: Yes, absolutely – look, it says so here.

Mrs Ferret: So I wouldn't have to have it dry-cleaned?

Brenda: No.

Mrs Ferret: And the colours won't run?

Brenda: No, madam.

Mrs Ferret: Shrinkage?

Brenda: No, it won't shrink.

Reassure suspicious customers

Suspicious customers are desperately in need of reassurance. They're terrified they're going to be caught out, and they leave no stone unturned to prevent this happening. They check and double-check everything, wanting to test your authority and reliability, your organisation, products or services, and your knowledge. It can be like a full-scale interrogation, but if you don't go along with it you'll lose the customer.

Don't hustle Mr Clam.

*So you think
you can cope
with customers?*

Mrs Ferret: But are you sure it won't?
Brenda: No, it says so here.
Mrs Ferret: You're *not* sure.
Brenda: Yes, I am. Look, here's the
    guarantee.
Mrs Ferret: So, it's non-shrinkable?
Brenda: Yes, madam.
Mrs Ferret: And that's guaranteed?
Brenda: Yes.
Mrs Ferret: And that's the guarantee?
Brenda: Yes.
Mrs Ferret: Supposing the guarantee
    shrinks?

That's Mrs Ferret all right, nosing and
sniffing around for faults and mistakes
and problems. She's suspicious of all the
things that can go wrong, *and* all the people she deals with, which is why she checks
and double checks and then checks again.
So, if you're not really expert . . .

Mrs Ferret: What's the airmail
    postage to Uganda?
Brian: Eight pence for half an ounce.
Mrs Ferret: You're quite sure?
Brian: Er . . . yes.
Mrs Ferret: You're absolutely sure?
Brian: Er . . . yes.
Mrs Ferret: Beyond any reasonable
    doubt?
Brian: Well, I think . . . it used to be.
Mrs Ferret: You're *not* sure.
Brian: Well, ex-Commonwealth . . .
Mrs Ferret: You said you were
    absolutely sure!
Brian: Well, I was . . .
Mrs Ferret: Oh, dear, and they can
    put a man on the moon.

With Mrs Ferret, you really need to be

an expert – because that sort of questioning soon rattles you if you're not. But if you do know your stuff, don't let her break you down. And don't let it rattle you if she starts checking up on you.

Mrs Ferret: So, you're sure it's washable?
Brenda: Yes, madam.
Mrs Ferret (*to another assistant*): That's right, is it? It is washable?
Assistant: Er, yes, madam.
Mrs Ferret: Oh, excuse me, are you the Manageress? Is this washable?

On the other hand, if she asks you something you don't know, don't pretend you do.

Mrs Ferret: How much is the postage to Chile?
Brian: Er . . . er . . . eleven pence for half an ounce.
Mrs Ferret: Are you sure?
Brian: Absolutely! Yes!
Mrs Ferret: Well, excuse me, are you in charge?
Manager: Yes, madam.
Mrs Ferret: Is that right, eleven pence to Chile?
Manager: No, madam, it's only eight pence.
Mrs Ferret: He told me it was eleven pence.
Manager: What?
Brian: Oh, Chile. I thought you said Chorley.
Manager: Eleven pence to Chorley?
Brian: Oh no.
Mrs Ferret: He's trying to do me out of three pence.

Be patient and honest

Don't let the persistent questioning rattle you. If they ask the same question three times, be sure and give the same answer each time. And never say, 'I've already told you that twice,' or they'll think you made the first two answers up and now you can't remember what you said. The keys to dealing with this sort of customer are patience and being prepared to admit that you don't know something instead of pretending that you do. It's better to go and find out than to be found out, and you can be sure Mrs Ferret will find you out if you prevaricate.

Sure it's alcohol-free . . .

If you're asked something you don't know, don't pretend you do.

So to cope with Mrs Ferret, stick to your guns. But if she asks you something you don't know, find out. Don't pretend you do. And then all is plain sailing with Mrs Ferret, provided you avoid one fatal error – the surefire, guaranteed way of losing Mrs Ferret as a customer.

Mrs Ferret: So I've got the choice between steamer, train, plane or coach.

Brian: Yes, madam.

Mrs Ferret: Now, let's just see if I've got it right. I can fly direct to Berne and then take the train or the coach, or I could fly to Cologne, take the steamer to Basle and then the train or coach, or I could take the cross-channel ferry to Boulogne, change at Strasbourg and another train to Berne, and then by coach if I felt like it, or I could go to Amsterdam and take the steamer the whole way down, or I could fly to Geneva and take the boat across to Lausanne and then by coach, or just fly to Basle and take the train to Berne.

Brian: That's it.

Mrs Ferret: Are there any other ways?

Brian: Well, I suppose you could take the hovercraft to Vienna, stroll across to Geneva, waterski across to Montreux and catch the train from there.

Mrs Ferret: No, I can't waterski.

Brian: Well, we'll scrub that one, then.

Mrs Ferret: Well, we've checked them all.

Brian: Yes – we – have.

Mrs Ferret: Yes, I think ... I think I'll

*So you think
you can cope
with customers?*

fly to Cologne, take the steamer to
Basle and then go by train.

Brian: Very good, madam.

Mrs Ferret: I'd just like to check a
few things.

Brian: Ah.

Mrs Ferret: Now, this is a day flight,
isn't it?

Brian: That's right, madam. Now,
which . . .

Mrs Ferret: That's second class on
the steamer?

Brian: Right. Now which day . . .

Mrs Ferret: Do I spend a night in
Cologne?

Brian: If you want to, madam.

Mrs Ferret: Oh, how much will that
cost me?

Brian: It's all down there, madam.
Now which . . .

Mrs Ferret: Now, that's two days on
the steamer.

Brian: It *is* there, madam. It is correct,
I promise you. Now, which day
would you like to travel, madam?
I'm sorry, but I have to go to lunch
in a couple of moments.

Mrs Ferret: Oh! Oh, well.

Brian: Which day, madam?

Mrs Ferret: Yes, well I'd like to think
about it.

Brian: But it's all down there,
madam . . . all the information. . .

Mrs Ferret: No, no, I'd rather think
about it.

Brian: We've been over it several
times.

Mrs Ferret: I'll see. I'll be in again.

Brian: Is there anything wrong?

Mrs Ferret: I'll be in *again*.

68

That was the classic mistake with Mrs Ferret. Trying to hurry her into a decision. That is fatal because she is suspicious of everybody and everything. And it's your job to remove those suspicions or she won't buy. Remove them patiently one by one . . . and if you hurry her, what does she think?

Mrs Ferret: (*to herself*): Why's he hurrying me? Why? He must have a reason. There must be something wrong. And he's trying to hide it by hurrying me. Oh no, no, no, no.

The only way to deal with Mrs Ferret properly is to give her all the time she needs. Deal patiently with each and every suspicion in turn.

Mrs Ferret: Good, yes, well. I'll take that one.
Brenda: Excellent, madam.
Mrs Ferret: Now, look, if these are my measurements, how many yards will I need?
Brenda: Four yards for each curtain, that makes eight yards, and then, if you want the patterns to match, an extra two yards.
Mrs Ferret: Two?
Brenda: To be sure they match.
Mrs Ferret: Look, is that correct? Two extra yards to make the patterns right? (*She asks another assistant.*)
Assistant: Yes, madam, if they're going to match.
Mrs Ferret: No, no, I only need eight yards.
Brenda: No, madam, you see you

Know your company procedures

Mrs Ferret is very keen on discounts, reductions, replacements and the rights of customers. She's also likely to be knowledgeable about your company's practices, because she'll have tried it on before. Just because it didn't work last time doesn't mean she won't try again. So you need to be as certain about company procedures as you are about your stock or the services you offer.

Be tactful and professional

Remember that all these awkward people are awkward because that is part of their lifestyle – it's got nothing to do with the fact that you work in a shop or service counter. They are awkward with everyone they meet, because that is the approach they always take in their dealings with people. So console yourself with the fact that the next person they meet will get similar treatment. You can't change their personality, so don't even try. Just deal with them tactfully and professionally.

*So you think
you can cope
with customers?*

want the pattern to start in the same
place . . .

She'll never believe you unless you show
her.

Brenda: Let me show you, madam.

There is one other way in which Mrs
Ferret tests your knowledge. She's
always on the look-out for a bargain.

Mrs Ferret: There's a mark on here.
Brian: Well, here's a clean one.
Mrs Ferret: Well, is there any reduction
on that one?
Brian: No I'm afraid not.
Mrs Ferret: There's only one of these.
Brian: Yes.
Mrs Ferret: And some of the stiches are
loose, so it's not full price, is it?
Brian: I'll have to see if there's another
one in stock, and if not I'll have to ask
a supervisor.

You've got to be an expert on company
procedures too.

Mrs Ferret takes an age to deal with,
but you can save time by leaving her on
her own. She's often happy to get on
with things unaided, so do this when you
can. She may take up a lot of time, but
it's the only way of dealing with her.

There's one particular reason why it's
worth spending a lot of time on Mrs
Ferret. All her friends know what she's
like, and how hard she is to satisfy, so
one long hard sell to Mrs Ferret will
often mean several short ones to her
friends.

All Mrs Ferret's friends know how hard she is to satisfy.

Golden rules

Make sure you know your stuff.

Don't try to put awkward customers down, use tact to build them up and flatter if necessary.

With taciturn customers, don't chatter at them – use short factual remarks.

If at first you don't succeed, move away and try again later.

With suspicious customers, make sure you know your stuff.

Deal with each suspicion or worry in turn and don't try to rush things.

Save time by leaving the customer on her own.

Quite apart from the awkward squad, there are some customers who have only the vaguest idea of what they want. They're not stupid, they just haven't had to consider this type of purchase before, and they will look to you as an expert to guide them.

If you get it wrong, you can be in trouble with the Sale of Goods Act but, worse that that, you will have alienated a customer. People who put their trust in you will come back again if you look after them – but if you don't, they stop being a customer and become a complainer.

Customer: I'm a little confused. I want to buy a present for my grandson. I thought perhaps a cassette-player.
Brian: Yes, sir. Portable or pocket-size?
Customer: Well, I don't know. To tell the truth I've never bought one before.
Brian: This is a popular model.
Customer: Does it work off batteries?
Brian: Yes. They're inside the box.
Customer: Thank you. I'll take it.
Brian: His grandson won't thank him for that. It's not even stereo.

Yes, Brian sold him a cassette-player. The customer has gone away happy, thinking that he has been well advised by an 'expert'. Only when he gets home and sees his grandson's face will he realise that he's made a mistake, but by that time it will be too late to swap the cassette-player and put right the damage in the grandfather's mind about the

5 'What do you want?', or 'I've never bought one of these before'

The customer needs your expertise

It's a classic mistake to assume that other people think and react like you, or that they have the same knowledge as you, just because they are the same age group and sex. If that was true, they would be doing your job instead of buying from you. They come to you because they want to use your expertise to help them, just as you got to a solicitor for his expertise when you need it.

73

*So you think
you can cope
with customers?*

way he was treated in the shop.

The problem with this customer was that he had a lack of knowledge. He wasn't an expert on what he was buying and therefore he was relying on Brian's expertise to help him. It would have been much better for all concerned if the conversation had gone like this:

Customer: I'm a little confused. I want to buy a present for my grandson. I thought perhaps a cassette-player.

Brian: Portable or pocket-size?

Customer: Well, I don't know. To tell the truth, I've never bought one before.

Brian: Well, the pocket-size ones are what the young people like nowadays. Let me show you some. This is a basic model. It's a good make, but not quite such high-quality sound as this one.

Customer: That looks all right. It's a little small, isn't it?

Brian: They're all small like this – and very good. But if you'd like something a little bigger, this one has the advantage of a radio as well.

Customer: That's a good idea.

You have to be a bit of an amateur psychologist. You need to unearth exactly what it is the customer requires and not just rely on his description of his requirements. You need to be an interpreter and use your expertise to help him. And you mustn't make assumptions. Every youth with long hair and scruffy jeans isn't a trouble-maker, and

'Twisty, pointy things', madam? – take your pick!

You need to unearth exactly what it is the customer requires and not just rely on her description of her requirements.

*So you think
you can cope
with customers?*

Don't assume a woman is a housewife

In today's world, just because a customer is female, you shouldn't assume that she is a housewife, any more than you should assume that all men know about cars or carpentry. It is particularly annoying for the professional woman to be treated like an idiot because she doesn't fit the domestic role model – especially when the person who is doing it clearly doesn't earn as much as she does.

every woman in her thirties isn't necessarily an experienced home-maker.

Take Ms Career. She's thirty-two and she's just got her master's degree in Business Studies. She's highly competent at her job, but she's spent all her life so far living with her parents or at university. Now she's got a highly paid job and she's bought a flat. And she needs some curtains.

Ms Career: Can you help me please? I need curtains.
Brenda: Certainly, madam. Where for?
Ms Career: Oh, er . . . everywhere.
Brenda: Everywhere?
Ms Career: Yes, everywhere. Bedroom, lounge, hall, dining-room, bathroom – everywhere. It's a new flat, you see, and it hasn't any curtains.
Brenda: I see, madam. Well, look, the bedroom curtains are over there, and the bathroom ones over there, and the others are here. You find the designs you like, then I'll get the right sizes from the stockroom.

That sounds all right so far, but Brenda has missed the uncertainty in Ms Career's voice. And she still isn't listening properly when Ms Career comes back.

Ms Career: These are rather nice. The colour's just right.
Brenda: Splendid, madam. Now, what size?
Ms Career: Er . . . well . . . the window is 56″ by 72″

N-E-E-D-L-E!

It is particularly annoying
for the professional woman
to be treated like an idiot.

*So you think
you can cope
with customers?*

Brenda: 72″ drop?
Ms Career: Er . . . drop? It's 72″ from
   top to bottom.
Brenda: Right, madam. Rufflette?
Ms Career: Er . . . yes, I suppose so.

Brenda really missed the clues there. So
it's no surprise when Ms Career comes
back the next day.

Ms Career: Those curtains I bought
   yesterday – they don't seem big
   enough. I couldn't actually put them
   up properly – the ring things didn't
   fit, but I pinned them up and they
   definitely weren't long enough *and*
   they didn't meet. Are you sure you
   gave me the right size?
Brenda: Well, the label says 56″ by
   72″, madam – let me measure in
   case they were packed wrongly. No,
   they're 56″ by 72″ all right. Perhaps
   you measured wrongly.
Ms Career: No, I checked that again.
   The window is 56″ by 72″, but these
   didn't come down far enough.
Brenda: Oh, I see, madam. You say
   the window is 72″, but the drop has
   to be more. You need at least 78″
Ms Career: Are you sure?
Brenda: Yes, madam, but you ought
   to measure again. Now, madam,
   you mentioned rings, but you did say
   rufflette yesterday.
Ms Career: No, *you* said rufflette. I
   thought that was the material.
Brenda: No, madam, it's the fixing
   tape. Now, you'd better measure
   again, and make sure what the
   fixings are, and . . .
Ms Career: No. I'll have my money

back please. Then I think I'll find someone to make some proper fitted curtains for me.

Brenda (*to another assistant as Ms Career goes out*): That's strange. You'd think a woman of that age would know about curtains, wouldn't you?

Now that's a pity, because that customer was prepared to buy several pairs of curtains, if only Brenda had heard the clues and hadn't jumped to conclusions. Maybe Doreen can do better.

Ms Career: Can you help me please? I need curtains.

Doreen: Certainly, madam. Where for?

Ms Career: Oh, er . . . everywhere.

Doreen: Everywhere, madam? Is it a new house?

Ms Career: Oh yes. Well, a new flat.

Doreen: Right, madam. None of your old ones fit, then?

Ms Career: I haven't any old ones. It's my first place – I've always been at home before.

Doreen: I see. Tell me, madam, have you ever bought curtains before? Do I detect a slight uncertainty?

Ms Career: Oh no, I've never bought curtains before. It isn't that difficult, is it? I mean, you do have ready-made ones, don't you? I don't have the time for sewing.

Doreen: Don't worry, madam, you won't need to sew. They're all ready to hang, all you have to do is put the hooks in.

Ms Career: Hooks?

Doreen: Yes, hooks. The curtains have a tape on the back at the top,

'What do you want?', or 'I've never bought one of these before'

Put yourself in the customer's position

Don't jump to conclusions. What may to you be the obvious way to do something may never occur to someone else – like the proper place to take measurements. It's only obvious to you because you actually know how to do it. Think of all the things you've done wrong the first time you tried, then put yourself in the customer's shoes to take another look at the situation you're dealing with.

*So you think
you can cope
with customers?*

with places to put the hooks. You
just hook them into the tape, then
over the curtain rail. Did you notice
what sort of rail it was? Round or
flat?

Ms Career: Oh yes, I noticed that. It
was flat, and about this wide.

Doreen: Like this?

Ms Career: Yes, that's it.

Doreen: Right, madam. These are the
hooks you need. I'll show you how
they go in when we've found the
curtains you like.

Ms Career: Thank you. I've never
had to do anything like this before –
my mother used to do it all.

Doreen is doing fine. She's getting the
information she needs from Ms Career,
and giving Ms Career the information
she needs without being patronising.

Doreen: Right, madam. Shall we start
with bedroom curtains?

Ms Career: Oh yes. I'd like something
nice and light and airy.

Doreen: I can do you a pale colour,
but I wouldn't advise a light fabric.
You need to keep the sun out first
thing in the summer, or you'll be
awake at four o'clock.

Ms Career: Oh, I didn't think of that.

Doreen: And you'll want them a good
length for the same reason. You
want the tops at least three inches
above the top of the window and
three inches below, and plenty of
width, or there'll be chinks of light
showing through the gaps.

Ms Career: Oh dear. It's all much
more complicated than I thought.

Doreen: Not really, madam – just a few little things that come with experience. I didn't know any of it until I joined this department, but even I soon caught on. Now, did you take some measurements?

Ms Career: Yes. The window is 56″ wide and 72″ high.

Doreen: Is that the glass or the outside of the frame?

Ms Career: The outside of the frame – so they'll want to be 78″ long then, won't they? And 60″ wide?

Doreen: Well, no, they want to be wider than that, especially if you want them to hang in folds – like this, look. We usually say the curtains should be nearly twice as wide as the window, so if you have a pair of 48″ by 78″, that should be just about right.

Ms Career: I see. I like these blue ones. Have you got them in that size?

Doreen: Yes . . . and I'll get you a copy of our booklet on curtains, in case there's anything else you need to know.

Ms Career: Thank you very much. I'll try these tonight and then I'll check the measurements in the lounge and come back for those tomorrow. Will you be here again?

Doreen: Yes, madam.

Ms Career: Good. I like to deal with someone who knows what they're doing.

So there we are – a happy customer, with the intention of coming back to buy from Doreen again. All it takes is a tuned ear and a few questions.

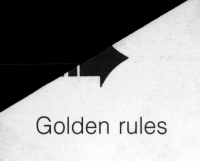

Golden rules

Don't make assumptions about a customer's knowledge

Listen for the clues.

Ask the relevant questions.

Give the information the customer needs without being patronising.

What many of us do not realise is that the way we behave towards customers affects the way they behave towards us. Behaviour actually breeds behaviour – helpful behaviour breeds happy relaxed customers, unhelpful behaviour breeds angry resentful complainers.

Consider Mr Hapless, who is getting ready to go on holiday when the doorbell rings.

Mr Hapless: Yes?

Mr Pilbury: Mr Hapless? You wanted a new extension socket?

Mr Hapless: Oh, I'd completely forgotten. I'm just going away on holiday . . .

Mr Pilbury: So I see. Anywhere nice?

Mr Hapless: Ephemera.

Mr Pilbury: Abroad, sunshine, eh?

Mr Hapless: Yes. So do you think you could come back another time?

Mr Pilbury: It'll only take me a minute. I promise I won't get in your way.

Mr Hapless: All right then, yes, come in. Thank you very much. It's up in my mother's bedroom, first on the left.

So that's Mr Hapless – an ordinary, pleasant, unassuming member of the public. Or is he? Sister Cartledge saw him in a different light – difficult and truculent, the sort of patient she could well do without.

Sister Cartledge: Next! Over there. Ephemerenza, right?

Mr Hapless: Yes.

Sister Cartledge: Roll your sleeve up.

6 If looks could kill, or the power of behaviour

Your behaviour will influence the customer

No one can ever see your motives, your thoughts, your attitudes or your feelings. People can only see the behaviour that results from these things. So it follows that other people's impressions of you have to be based on the behaviour they see, as well as the words they hear. Your behaviour is like a beacon sending out signals to all the people with whom you have dealings. The signals you send are vital because they are a major influence on the reactions of the other person and they can help or hinder every transaction.

*So you think
you can cope
with customers?*

Mr Hapless: Er, is this absolutely necessary? I do find injections very . . .

Sister Cartledge: You think health regulations are there for fun, do you?

Mr Hapless: No, I was only asking . . .

Sister Cartledge (*looking at her watch*): Yes.

Mr Hapless: Well, do you think perhaps there's a pill I might be able to take?

Sister Cartledge: Don't you think I'd give it to you if there were? Now, do you want this injection or not? I'm a busy woman.

Mr Hapless: And a very rude one – you ought to be more polite.

Sister Cartledge: I treat you just the same as everyone else. (*She sticks the needle in.*)

Mr Hapless: Aaaaaagh! Cow!

You might think Mr Hapless has had a personality change – and so he had – the personality of Mr Pilbury and the personality of Sister Cartledge. It was the different behaviour of each of the two towards him that caused Mr Hapless to behave in two such contrasting ways.

It's a common misconception that behaviour is something you're born with, but that isn't true. It's not a constant, like your gender or the colour of your eyes; it's a variable, like a hat you wear. It's a performance – a performance you choose to put on.

Which doesn't mean that all the customers you meet will be all sweetness and light. They may be smarting from

Encourage the customer to talk

If you ask someone an open question, nine times out of ten they will give you an answer. And if you smile and nod your head while they are answering, they will say more than they would if you had kept your head still. There's nothing like encouragement to keep the words coming.

their last encounter and be touchy before you start. Like poor Mr Hapless, who had to go from Sister Cartledge to take back a faulty pair of shoes.

Mr Welt: I do apologise. I'll send them back to the manufacturers at once.

Mr Hapless: But I'm going on holiday in a minute. I want them replaced now!

Mr Welt: I'm sorry, sir, but we don't stock summer lines at this time of the year.

Mr Hapless: Why not?

Mr Welt: There's no demand for sandals so late in the season.

Mr Hapless: But there's a pair in the window;

Mr Welt: Yes, sir . . . they're for display only.

Mr Hapless: Get them out.

Mr Welt: They're . . . not . . . your . . . size.

Mr Hapless: How do you know?

Mr Welt: I put them there.

Mr Hapless: I want to see the Manager.

Mr Welt: I am the Manager.

Mr Hapless: Then heaven help the shoe business. Keep your perishing sandals and drop dead!

Mr Welt got that all wrong, because he made one simple mistake. He didn't realise that he could choose how to react to Mr Hapless's behaviour. Instead of reacting to rudeness by being awkward, he could have chosen to be pleasant in order to get Mr Hapless to be pleasant back. The professional approach is

There's no excuse for bad behaviour

People who behave badly often have plausible excuses. 'You must take me as you find me' really means 'I'm going to behave as I always do even if you don't like it.' 'I'm too old to change my ways – you can't teach an old dog new tricks' really means 'I can't be bothered to modify my behaviour, so I'll argue that it isn't possible and that will provide the perfect excuse.'

*So you think
you can cope
with customers?*

often the productive approach. Let's see where that moment of choice came.

Mr Hapless: But there's a pair in the window.
Mr Welt: Yes, sir . . . they're for display only.
Mr Hapless: Get them out.

There! That's where Mr Welt chose to snap back, when he could have said:

Mr Welt: Well, we don't normally sell the display shoes, sir, but . . . why don't you take a seat, and I'll see if they're your size.
Mr Hapless: Oh, all right.
Mr Welt: The colour may be a bit faded, but at least we'll get you off on your holiday with something to wear!
Mr Hapless: Yes, yes . . . thank you.

You see? A changed man. Had Mr Welt understood the power of behaviour, Mr Hapless would have left his shop a changed man.

Mind you, he wouldn't have entered it in such a bad mood if Sister Cartledge hadn't been so obnoxious. She might have been a little more patient, a little more understanding, perhaps gentler. More professional.

Sister Cartledge: Good morning! Mr Hapless, isn't it?
Mr Hapless: Yes, that's right.
Sister Cartledge: Let me take your coat.
Mr Hapless: Do you think this is absolutely necessary? I do find

injections very . . .

Sister Cartledge (*giving him a reassuring touch on the arm*): Don't worry, Mr Hapless, a lot of people hate injections. I tell you what, you count to ten and I'll be finished before you even get there.

You see, a simple technique – a smile, the mention of his name, a touch on the arm, and he's a different human being. She used her behaviour to help that transaction, but you can also use behaviour to hinder.

It was to Mr Figgis's counter at the post office that Mr Hapless came shortly after his bad encounter with Mr Welt.

Mr Figgis (*to a colleague*): So I said, if that's what you think we're made of, you can think again, John. Well, you've got to let them know who's boss, haven't you.

Mr Hapless: Excuse me, I've come to collect this pension.

Mr Figgis: One moment. (*He picks up some forms, taps them on the desk to make a tidy bundle of them, finds an elastic band and straps them together.*) Can I help you?

Mr Hapless: Yes, look, I've come to collect my mother's pension today, now, this minute – you see I'm off on holiday.

Mr Figgis: Why hasn't your mother come to collect it herself?

Mr Hapless: Well, it's all properly authorised and everything.

The phone rings and Mr Figgis answers it.

Your behaviour creates an impression

People gain a general impression of you from a combination of your facial expression and head movements, your gestures with your hands and arms, and the rest of your body including your legs. They will tend to see you as defensive if you avoid looking at them, clench your hands or cross your arms, keep rubbing an eye, ear or your nose, lean away from them, cross your legs or swivel your feet towards the door. They will tend to see you as anxious if you blink frequently, lick your lips, keep clearing your throat, put your hand over your mouth while you are speaking, tug at your ear, fidget in your chair or move your feet up and down.

*So you think
you can cope
with customers?*

Mr Figgis: Yes? No, no, no. (*He puts it
down and looks at Mr Hapless again.*)
Now, can I help you?

Mr Hapless: I've come to collect this
pension.

Mr Figgis: Pensions? Not here –
second window down!

Mr Hapless: Call yourself a public
service? You're a public disgrace, I
mean, I wouldn't buy a penny stamp
from this post office if it was the last
one on earth!

Let's just look at all the things Mr Figgis
did wrong.

He didn't acknowledge Mr Hapless's
presence while he kept him waiting.

He didn't have to keep him waiting –
a lot of that was just one-upmanship, to
make the customer think he was rather
low on the list of priorities.

He didn't look at Mr Hapless while
he was speaking to him.

When he said 'Can I help you?' it
looked as if he meant 'Can I hinder
you?' he was so busy doing something
else.

He looked bored and unreceptive
when he was listening.

Poor Mr Hapless. After that little
encounter, he really wasn't in the mood
for a smart-Alec porter at the station.

Mr Tanner: Yes, guv. What can I do
for you? Short-back-and-sides?
Extra hole in your belt? Ear-piercing
while you wait?

Mr Hapless: Is this the airport train?

Mr Tanner: No, guv. Cor – you're
gonna need a holiday by the time
you get there with all that lot!

Be friendly and welcoming – lean forward and use open gestures, not closed ones.

Mr Hapless: Then could you tell me where . . .

Mr Tanner: Cor blimey, what do you think I am? Encyclopedicka Britannica? Any questions, try the Enquiries Office.

Mr Hapless: I see, and where's that?

Mr Tanner: Well, they'll tell you that when you get there. Ha ha ha!

It's all very well to have a joke, but not at the expense of other people.

And to cap it all, when he got to the airport, Mr Hapless's plane was delayed. At least Lindy was able to handle him professionally, despite the fact that she'd had a bust-up with her boyfriend the previous night and she'd just been told her cat had been run over by a car.

Lindy: Good afternoon, sir, could I please have your ticket. And if you'd like to put your cases on the scales . . . Ah, Mr Hapless, I'm afraid I have some bad news for you.

Mr Hapless: Oh, no . . . what?

Lindy: I'm sorry to say your flight has been cancelled.

Mr Hapless: What?

Lindy: Yes, the plane coming from Ephemera has been delayed, so all the passengers for flight 201 are going to be transferred to flight 203 first thing tomorrow morning.

Mr Hapless: But this is outrageous!

Lindy: It must be terribly upsetting, sir.

Mr Hapless: I shall phone the Managing Director.

Don't use aggressive behaviour

People will tend to see you as aggressive and overbearing if you stare at them, raise your eyebrows in disbelief, look at them over the top of your spectacles, or smile in a 'heard it all before' way; or if you point at them, thump your fist on the table, stride around or stand while they are seated; or, if you are seated, lean right back in your chair with your hands behind your head and your legs splayed.

*So you think
you can cope
with customers?*

Using body language

If you want to seem friendly and co-operative, look at the other person's face, smile and nod when they are talking, have open hands and uncrossed arms and legs, lean forward slightly or move closer to them. If you want to appear confident, look into their eyes, don't blink, keep your hands away from your face, stay still and don't make sudden movements. If you want to appear thoughtful, tilt your head to one side, stroke your chin or pinch the bridge of your nose, lean forward to speak and back to listen and keep your legs still.

Lindy: Well, if you'd like to see our Passenger Liaison Officer, she is waiting in the Ambassador Lounge to help anyone with a particular problem . . .

Mr Hapless: Oh well.

Lindy: Do you live near the airport?

Mr Hapless: No I don't.

Lindy: In that case we can provide free transport to and from home . . .

Mr Hapless: I'm not going all the way home again.

Lindy: I see, you'd prefer to stay nearer the airport.

Mr Hapless: That's right.

Lindy: Of course, well, we can provide accommodation for you at the Airport Hotel . . . or if you'd prefer somewhere cosier?

Mr Hapless: Yes, please.

Lindy did all that right. In spite of her personal problems, in spite of a slightly awkward passenger, and in the face of a tricky situation, she remembered that you can use your behaviour to help a transaction in two ways – verbally and visually.

Verbally

Rule one: acknowledge people as soon as possible.

Rule two: apologise for any delay.

Rule three: use people's names – wherever you can.

Rule four: confirm that you're listening – don't just stand there, say something.

Rule five: check you've understood and agree the next step – and give people a choice where you can.

Visually

Rule six: be friendly and welcoming.
Rule seven: look at people and be attentive – nod and, where appropriate, take written notes.
Rule eight: Lean forward and use open gestures, not closed ones.

A faultless performance from Lindy. It was nobody's fault that the car she provided to take Mr Hapless to his hotel broke down some half-mile from its destination, and Mr Hapless, who had been goaded, frustrated and enraged for the greater part of the day, arrived sweating and fuming at the charming country hotel where he had been booked in at the airline's epense.

Mr Manners: And to what do we owe this visit, Mr Hapless? Business or pleasure?

Mr Hapless: Business – as in mind your own.

Mr Manners: Oh. I do beg your pardon, sir. I'd like to point out that while you are our guest, it would be our pleasure . . .

Mr Hapless: Just a minute. I have had enough of this flannel to last me a lifetime. I've had it up to here, I mean I am sick of 'Yes, Mr Hapless,' 'No, Mr Hapless,' 'Three bags full, Mr Hapless.' I've got the message, you know, I know what's being said to me. I understand these things, you know. Listen, why don't you people just say what you mean, why don't you say, 'Go and jump in the lake'? That's what you mean, isn't it? Go on, say it, say it!

You can change your behaviour

Behaviour isn't an automatic reflex such as breathing. You had to learn how to behave with people and there is nothing to stop you unlearning and replacing any of your behaviours. The secret of success is to start thinking about the choices you have instead of behaving in an unthinking way. The trick is to decrease the behaviours that hinder and increase the behaviours that help. You only need keep an eye on your audience to see how each piece of behaviour is being received and you'll soon find out which is which.

Mr Manners: Why don't you go and jump in the lake, Mr Hapless?
Mr Hapless: Right, I will.

Oh dear, Mr Manners was faced with the ultimate test – a completely impossible customer. The sort you cannot live with. Yet he did the unforgiveable, the unprofessional – he cracked. At the moment of choice, he chose the wrong behaviour.

If looks could kill, or the power of behaviour

Golden rules

Behaviour breeds behaviour – remember that the way people behave towards you is influenced by the way you behave towards them.

You can choose your behaviour. Your behaviour is not something you are born with; it's something you choose every time you deal with the public; and how you choose will help or hinder every single transaction.

You can use your behaviour to help a transaction: **verbally**, by greeting people and using their names; and **visually**, with an attentive look and gesture.

Everyone has to deal with complaints occasionally. But when they do crop up, it's a good idea to bear in mind someone who has to spend his life dealing with 'complaints' – a doctor. Because most of the rules a doctor has learnt to apply when he's handling 'complaints' – his practical do's and don't's – also hold true for anyone handling customer complaints.

Mr Richards: In all my twenty-seven years in business – and you can ask anyone, I've been dealing with these machines longer than you or your precious Mr Fanshawe – in all my experience I've never had the aggravation that I've had with this damn FB Two-One-Two of yours. Damn near at a standstill we've been here, a complete standstill, could just as well have shut up shop and sent everybody home as far as getting any satisfaction from your Head Office is concerned. Letter after letter I've sent them – a fortune on postage . . .

They tend to overwhelm you with all sort of elaborate detail and misplaced emphasis. But think back to the last time you went to the doctor's and remember his response. He's attentive. He listens. Because he knows from experience the dangers of interrupting too readily.

Mr Richards: And when I wrote to your Head Office and pointed out what was wrong, what do I get back? An invoice. A flaming invoice! Now I ask you, when you write

7 Prescription for complaints

Complaints are common

Complaints are common to every business. People make mistakes. Customers and suppliers alike can be wrong, so complaints are bound to be made. What is important is how well they will be dealt with. A customer who complains is giving you a chance to put things right. It's the disgruntled customer who doesn't complain who is worse, for he just makes up his mind to go somewhere else in future. There is nothing like a well-handled complaint for welding two parties together in business.

complaining about a machine's performance, you do not expect to get a bleeding invoice. I tell you, I was so livid I sat down and I wrote them that if they did not send me an engineer, an experienced qualified engineer . . .

Joe: A-ha! Got you!

Mr Richards: Eh?

Joe: You nasty little blighter!

Mr Richards: I beg yours?

Joe: That's where your trouble is, squire. We're earthing, aren't we. We're shorting across, that's what we're doing. That's where your trouble is, in your make-and-break.

Mr Richards: You must be joking.

Joe: Not to worry. If I take out that whole component, I can bypass the other terminal, replace it with the new component and we're in business. Can you spare this machine for the next hour or so?

Mr Richards: What do you mean, spare it for an hour or so? I don't need the damn thing at all!

Joe: Eh?

Mr Richards: Don't you listen to what people say to you?

Joe: Of course I listen. I mean, you've been complaining about the performance of your FB Two-One-Two.

Mr Richards: Because it's the wrong size! It should never have been recommended in the first place. I wanted someone to advise me on the installation of your One-One-Eight!

It is easy to 'switch off' when somebody's rabbiting on – and on and on. But where a complaint's concerned, hearing him not only saves you from an over-hasty diagnosis – it gives you an opportunity of summing your man up. Learning something about *him*.

So, for both customer and patient – the first prescription for alleviating the complaint is simply – **listen**. Merely allowing the complainer to unburden himself not only reduces the tension, it gives *you* information and rids *him* of some of his stored-up anxieties and fears.

Because there is an element of fear behind this going-on-and-on. He can never be quite certain that after he's said everything he's mentally rehearsed, after he's poured it all out, he won't hear something nasty when he stops talking.

Mr Richards: So what do you think, doctor?
Doctor: Hopeless!

Or in the customer situation –

Joe (*shaking his head*): Yeah, well, that's your tough luck, nothing we can do about it.

The first words that a person with a complaint wants to hear are words of sympathy, or concern. One sympathetic phrase is enough to dispose of the dreaded 'that's your tough luck' fantasy. It doesn't amount to an apology and it helps to defuse the situation. However:

Miss Reid: Such a lovely handbag. Tt–tt–tt . . .
Mr Burton: What does *that* mean?

99

*So you think
you can cope
with customers?*

Listen calmly to complaints

Very few people are constant complainers. For the majority, making a complaint is a major exercise. The cause of the complaint has probably given them a lot of grief already – a leaking washing-machine, a fridge that gets hot instead of cold, a late delivery or a mistake on a bank statement. On top of that, many people are afraid of complaining – they are subconsciously afraid that they will be accused of lying or making a fuss about nothing. This often makes them start off in an unnaturally aggressive manner. Once you've listened to the customer, allowed her to let off steam, got the details down correctly and sympathised with the inconvenience, the chances are that you will have cooled the customer down and put her in a frame of mind to seek a solution.

Miss Reid: What, sir?

Mr Burton: That 'tt–tt'.

Miss Reid: Well, such a beautiful article does need a certain delicacy in handling.

Mr Burton: Delicacy in handling! I told you what happened . . .

Miss Reid: Yes. Yes, you did. Tt–tt–tt. (*To herself:*) These people will do these things.

The 'it's your own fault' response may be quite valid, but imagine what would happen if a doctor allowed himself the luxury of taking that line.

Mr Burton: . . . across the whole of my lower abdomen! You do understand what I mean, doctor?

Doctor: Of course I understand. I'm a doctor, aren't I?

Mr Burton: What do you think happened?

Doctor: Well, you overate.

Mr Burton: I think it was the rock salmon. It set up an allergic syndrome. I was up for two nights with it, doctor. Agony. On Tuesday night I never thought I'd see morning.

Doctor: What did you expect, stuffing your belly like that? I'll tell you what your allergic syndrome is, Mr Burton. Good old-fashioned gluttony.

That's not really helping to soothe the patient's anxieties – a lecture, when what he's most obviously craving is reassurance. In the consulting-room, it's easy enough to appreciate how unproductive that attacking approach is – even though it may be heartfelt and even, possibly, accurate. And when it's applied to the customer situation:

Miss Reid: Well, can I put it to you, sir, that's sometimes it's a question of knowing *how* to look after good things.
Mr Burton: She never had it long enough to look after! First time she goes out, the leather stitching gives!
Miss Reid: Oh? You have a knowledge of leatherwork, do you, sir? In the trade, are you?
Mr Burton: No, no, of course not. I'm in wholesale plumbing accessories.
Miss Reid: Then may I ask on what basis you're alleging that the fault lies in our stitching?

Whatever he felt when he came in has been aggravated a hundredfold because he feels he's been put in the wrong for even venturing to complain – exactly the way a patient would react if a doctor made him feel he had no right to be ill. Which emphasises the second prescription for dealing with complaints: **after you've kept quiet and listened to the complaint, don't come out fighting.**

Sympathise. Express concern. Don't allow *his* hostilities to rub off on you – make allowance for them. A person with a complaint may appear to be spoiling for a fight, but deep down he wants a friend, not an enemy. So acknowledge his problem.

Mr Downs: Yes, yes, yes. Yes, I can

*So you think
you can cope
with customers?*

Don't justify

If the Distribution Manager of the
ABC Company rings to enquire
why his deliveries have not
arrived, telling him you are three
drivers short because of sickness
is not the answer he is looking for.
That's falling into the justification
trap. If you knew his deliveries
were going to be late, you should
have called him first to warn him.
Justification usually involves telling
people about your problems.
They're not interested in your
problems – they just want to know
what you are going to do to help
them solve theirs.

see how awkward it must have been
for you. Embarrassing, too, I should
have thought.

Mr Lever: Made me look a right idiot.
That's why I want to make
absolutely sure it never happens
again.

Mr Downs: Yes. Of course you do.
And so do we. We are as concerned
about it as you are.

Mr Lever: Which you have every right
to be. A large sum of money like
that – and don't forget, my chap
went to the trouble of getting special
clearance for that cheque – but
when my bank statement arrives,
blow me, no indication that it's been
credited to my account anywhere.

Mr Downs: Tt–tt–tt.

Mr Lever: Now what I want to hear
from you, Mr Downs, is an
assurance that this isn't going to be
a recurrent problem.

Mr Downs: What you'd like, Mr
Lever, is to feel free from any
uncertainties about future
statements from us. May I say that I
understand your state of mind
completely. Not only do I
understand it – let me tell you
something – I *live* with it. Those
damn computers – I'd hate to tell
you how many times I find myself
worrying about the figures they send
out. It's not as though you can rely
on the staff to get it right for you
any more . . .

That's a pity. Just when he was
doing well, Mr Downs blew it. He
allowed expressing sympathy to shade

off into appealing for sympathy – what's called 'justifying'. The hard fact is, when someone has a complaint, it's a cure he wants to hear about, not the causes.

Mr Lever: Oogh! That's it, doctor, that's the place.

Doctor (*wearily*): Same trouble as last time. Stress. Modern civilisation – God, how I hate it.

Mr Lever: It seems to be coming on often recently.

Doctor: Well, it's a stress condition! What can you expect? The pace we all live at today, what can anybody expect?

Mr Lever: I thought perhaps you might have something you could give me. I've heard there's a new painkiller on the marker. I thought perhaps you might . . .

Doctor: Oh, there are painkillers, there are tranquillisers, there are sedatives. But what are we doing? Papering over the cracks! Is that what I've spent fifteen years practising medicine for?

A doctor who drowns his patients' troubles with his own is helping neither himself nor his patient. When someone is waiting for a cure for *his* complaint, the one thing he's not interested in is someone else's problems.

When action is called for, don't waste time in self-defence, in appealing for sympathy or in apportioning blame. **Don't 'justify'.** However great the provocation, justifying is a luxury you can't afford at this stage. After listening and

I'm afraid your travel documents were prepared by a young man who thankfully has since left. As a matter of fact he appears in this old promotional video and, as you can see, he doesn't look at all bright, does he?

When action is called for, don't waste time in self-defence.

expressing sympathy, the next step must be to move, as any good doctor will tell you, into diagnosis and remedy.

This means **acquiring more information**, asking questions – the *right* questions, in the right way.

Mr Newly: And it was your people who said the tickets would be at the airport. A young lady sitting right where you are now. 'The tickets will be at the airport,' she says. And what happens when I get there? Blank faces. They'd never even heard of them. And while we were arguing the toss, the Frankfurt plane up and left and I was stranded.

Mrs Harper: Oh, I'm so sorry. That must have been awful.

Mr Newly: It certainly hasn't happened before.

Mrs Harper: Well, we'll have to see what we can do to put things right.

Mr Newly: The only way you can put things right is get me to Frankfurt in time for my conference.

Mrs Harper: In that case, Mr Newly, can I see your form RP 7102?

Mr Newly: My what?

Mrs Harper: RP 7102.

Mr Newly: Oh, for heaven's sake. Now look, I am not interested in forms and documents. Just get me to Frankfurt.

Mrs Harper: Yes, but I can't do that without your RP 7102 details.

Mr Newly: Oh you can't! Right! A quick phone call then. My company puts all its travel through you people, we'll just see about altering that.

Don't take complaints personally

The problem with complaints is similar to the problem with awkward customers. Those of us who receive complaints are inclined to take them as a personal slight. Consequently we are inclined to over-react and become defensive. Try to think of a complaint as a cry for help. It is essential that the first words the customer hears are words of sympathy, but this sympathy needs to be handled carefully. You mustn't overwhelm the customer with excessive admissions that it is your fault. You may be admitting legal liability when the fault actually lies elsewhere. So your expression of sympathy needs to be limited. You sympathise with the fact that the person has cause for a complaint, but you do not necessarily accept the blame.

*So you think
you can cope
with customers?*

When the way you ask your questions
gives the customer the impression that
he has become an object of official
interrogation he resents it. It looks as if
you are side-stepping his complaint, or
marking time on it. So how much better
if that question had been put in such a
way as to make the customer feel he was
helping to provide the solution.

Mr Newly: Get me on a plane to
    Frankfurt in time for my conference.
Mrs Harper: Of course, Mr Newly.
    What time is that conference?
Mr Newly: Noon tomorrow. I warn
    you, if I miss it, your company's
    going to be in a lot of trouble.
Mrs Harper: We'll get you there, but
    it would help considerably if I could
    just see your travel docket. If you
    haven't got it, it doesn't matter, I
    can always get the details from the
    files. But the more corners we can
    cut this end, the faster I can confirm
    your new booking.

A customer who complains is giving you
a chance. A chance to put things right.
And the first positive move that he sees
you make in that direction is when you
ask questions. So it matters how the
questions are asked, and in what form
they are put to him. Then – when you've
got *all* the information you require –
agree a course of action.

Mrs Harper: Now, if your conference
    is at noon tomorrow, what time
    would you like to get to Frankfurt?
Mr Newly: Well, I have to get to the
    hotel, have a shower, make some

phonecalls . . .

Mrs Harper: There's a plane here that would get you there at 10.15.

Mr Newly: Yes, that ought to do it.

The emphasis in agreeing a course of action is on the word 'agree'. Because, as any doctor will tell you, if a patient's mind is to be put at rest, the course of treatment suggested must be one he considers appropriate. So the final course of action must be agreed to be the most appropriate remedy.

Mrs Mason: I want my money back and that electric cooker taken out.

Mr Gorman: I don't blame you, it must have been a dreadful experience.

Mrs Mason: Absolutely awful. The smell! The mess!

Mr Gorman: Let's see if I've got down correctly what happened. You set the electric timer for the cooker to start cooking in thirty minutes' time, and then you left the kitchen . . .

Mrs Mason: Then I left the kitchen, forgot all about it, and suddenly there was this awful smell of burning! When I rushed back, what did I find? The wretched thing had started cooking right away. Everything ruined. Talk about burnt offerings. All that food ruined, to say nothing of the pots and pans. I want that whole rotten cooker taken out and my money back.

Mr Gorman: Well, shall we see what's involved. Would you like to sit down?

Mrs Mason: I brought all the papers

Ask for information about complaints

Asking questions is designed to do two things. Firstly, to give you more detailed information about the specific complaint so that you can put this in perspective against, say, what the machine was supposed to do or the services you were supposed to offer. Secondly, to help you see a way through to a possible solution to the problem. Make sure the questions you ask are open-ended questions, ones which will give a descriptive response.

back so you can see just how much it cost me.

Mr Gorman: Right. Now then, the only thing to be decided is . . . what's the best way we can help you?

Mrs Mason: Take it out of my home. That's the best thing you can do. Give me a cooker that cooks.

Mr Gorman: Let's take a look at the range we can offer at the moment, shall we?

So far, he's followed the prescriptions to the letter. He's listened, sympathised, hasn't attempted to justify, asked the right questions the right way. But now, he must remedy her complaint with a course of action that not only repairs the damage, but also meets *her* requirements.

Mr Gorman: Ah, this is the one you bought, isn't it? May I ask why you chose that one? I mean, I can see it's a nice cooker, but any other reason?

Mr Mason: Well, because of the timing-thing. It seemed so convenient. If the wretched thing only worked.

Mr Gorman: Now, what occurs to me, Mrs Mason, is that you might prefer it if I could put things right without taking the cooker out, upsetting your whole kitchen. It might only be a small fault, you see.

Mrs Mason: The timer, that's what it is.

Mr Gorman: Exactly. That's what we've got to correct, isn't it. Now supposing I send along one of our service engineers to replace it? After all, it is under guarantee.

Mrs Mason: If you knew how much time I waste hanging about waiting for electricians and plumbers who promise to come and never turn up.

Mr Gorman: All right. Let's make that a firm booking, shall we? Any particular day?

Mrs Mason: Tuesday might be all right. About three in the afternoon?

Mr Gorman: All right. Tuesday. Let's make that a firm booking, shall we? Tuesday at 3 p.m.

The mutually agreed remedy is the one that satisfies the customer's sense of grievance. And by handling the complaint suitably, your relationship with the customer can become even better than it was before. Which means there's one more rule to be observed, the one that comes *after* the customer has left.

Mr Gorman (*on the telephone*): George, about that electric timer for Mrs Mason. Yes. Will you make sure your engineer gets down there at 3 p.m. on Tuesday. Will you see to that? Jolly good. Thanks, George.

The final prescription for treating any complaint is to **check that the course of action is carried out.** Follow it up, implement it, ensure that it's all been done.

Mr Gorman: Hello, Mrs Mason. Yes, I just wanted to make sure the service engineer had got to you as arranged. He's there now? Oh fine, then your troubles are all over, aren't they?

Check that agreements are carried out

As is so often the case when something goes wrong, it is inclined to go very wrong before it gets better. So it is vital from your point of view that if you agreed with the customer that something would happen by a certain date, you check that it has happened. In a sense, it is the pre-emptive strike. You get in first before the customer rings you to say, 'What the — is going on?'

Golden rules

Learn to listen – hear the complaint right through.

Make sure your first response is words of sympathy.

Don't justify it, or try to apportion blame.

Collect the further facts you need by asking appropriate questions.

Agree a course of action.

Follow that course of action through to completion.

The commonest cause of customer complaints is faulty equipment. Even if they are not actually faulty, older items need regular maintenance and repairs. In either case, the customer needs a service engineer. In some companies he's known as a maintenance man. Officially, that is. In all too many cases he also has the unofficial title of 'Unsalesman'.

Meet our hero, Charlie Jenkins. On second thoughts, don't bother. Charlie Jenkins is Unsalesman of the year – one of the dominant figures of our industrial community. It's a shame really how no one has ever given him the recognition he deserves. In his own field, he's unbeatable. There isn't a salesman born who can survive against him. With one sentence, he can undo a month's patient selling.

Charlie: Who sold you this, then?

Mind you, it's easy for salesmen to blame it all on Charlie. They sow the dreams, he reaps the nightmares. People go to a salesman with stars in their eyes. They send for Charlie when there are six inches of water on the floor. Selling is about the lovely things that will happen tomorrow – service is about the awful thing that happened this morning.

Customers aren't always in the happiest frame of mind when they meet Charlie. They're often distressed, and sometimes they're very angry. When he started in this job, Charlie tried resisting the attack and standing up for the company – but if a man wants to keep his self-respect and have a quiet life

Be an ambassador for your company

Sales people sow the dreams about the lovely things that will happen tomorrow; the serviceman reaps the nightmares – it's him the customer sends for when something awful has happened. Anyone can start in the job trying to resist attacks and defend the company, but it's all too easy to wind up exhausted and deflect the attacks on to the product. If that doesn't work, you can blame the customer, or you can lay into Head Office, the organisation, 'them'. And finally, you can shoot down the salesperson, depicting him or her as a liar, a shark, a purveyor of dud goods designed solely to make your life hell. Clearly, that isn't the way your company wants you to operate. It would far rather you were an ambassador, not a hatchetman.

Customers aren't always in the happiest frame of mind when they meet Charlie.

there is a limit. Charlie reached his limit quite quickly, and ever since then he's been deflecting the attack instead. The product is the first target he deflects it on to.

Charlie: 'Allo, Mrs Thomas. I'm from Eldridge's.

Mrs Thomas: Oh, thank goodness you're here, it's a terrible state in there. I don't know what's happened to it, I really don't. Look at the water – I'll have to clean the whole . . .

Charlie: Oh dear. It's a B35. We have more trouble with these . . .

Mrs Thomas: Yes, well there's water all over the floor, and the lid's jammed.

Charlie: Yes, well it would, wouldn't it? Look at that – shouldn't be there. I mean, it should be round here where you can see it.

Mrs Thomas: Why don't they put it there, then?

Charlie: 'Cos they can't get it in the box when they're packing it. I ask you, there, look at that there next to the adjuster. You could lose a finger in there. They've only got to put a flange across. Course, this is the old model. Mind you, the new one's not exactly . . . still. Well, better have a look at it, I suppose. Trouble is, to service these properly, you need to be out of the Book of Revelations.

Mrs Thomas: The Book of Revelations?

Charlie: Yes, you need two heads, four arms, and seven fingers on each. I mean, I ask you, you didn't get this trouble with the old B3 you know.

'Who sold you this, then?

*So you think
you can cope
with customers?*

Mrs Thomas: Didn't you?

Charlie: No . . . marvellous model that was, marvellous. Course, they don't make them like that any more. Lasted too long. Still, this is a nice colour, isn't it?

Mrs Thomas: Well, can you do anything?

Charlie: Well, I can fix it, I suppose. Course, in a couple of weeks – still, you could be lucky.

But the product is only one of the casualties when Charlie gets to work. Sometimes it's the customer who suffers.

Charlie: What have you been doing with this?

Mr Mild: Er . . . nothing, it just started to sort of . . .

Charlie: The people up the road don't have any trouble with theirs, you know. Your competitors, aren't they?

Mr Mild: Ah, yes. Do you think you'll get it fixed in time for the next shift?

Charlie: When was the last time you adjusted the splinge on this? Have you got the manual? That's the book that tells you how to use this without damaging it beyond repair. Anyway, what exactly happened?

Mr Mild: Oh, well, it . . . it just started to make a noise.

Charlie: You didn't think to lift the cowling? What sort of noise? A grating or a crunching or a high-pitched squeaking or a harsh metallic scratching or a hollow full-throated humming or a dry reedy sputtering falsetto squealing or a plangent stridulous crescendoing

Be tolerant of your customers

Customers can be unbelievably stupid and ignorant. So what can we do? Prohibit them from buying the equipment until they pass a test? Punish them for mishandling it or failing to make elementary adjustments? Refuse to repair it until they sign up for a seven-day maintenance course? Or do we want to stay in business? Why not be as indulgent about their weaknesses as we'd like them to be about ours? Customers don't like being ticked off and humiliated any more than we do, and customers have the option of taking their custom to a supplier who leaves their self-respect intact.

droning counter-tenor snorting or . . . ?

Mr Mild: It was a sort of harsh metallic sound.

Charlie: What, steady or pulsating or measured or intermittent or seasonal or cyclical or rhythmic?

Mr Mild: It was pulsating. Evenly.

Charlie: Staccato?

Mr Mild: No, not staccato.

Charlie: Loud?

Mr Mild: Yes. Does that mean anything in particular?

Charlie: Course not. Could be anything. How long did you let it run after you heard these noises?

Mr Mild: Oh, about five minutes, and then . . .

Charlie: You're joking.

Mr Mild: Ah, here's the manual. Do you think you will manage to get it done by six?

Charlie: I could have done if you'd called me straight away. It'll be eight now.

When he's finished laying the blame on the customer, Charlie can always fall back on another victim – the organisation, Head Office, 'them'.

Charlie: Ah, I'll get on to them. It'll be a few weeks, possibly months, but I'll do what I can. Yeah, yeah, let me see if I can get something done for you. (*He picks up the telephone and dials.*) Oh, George, have you got any of those splicers? No, no, not those things, we haven't used them for years. No, you know, these things I've been asking you for, I mean this

Don't be negative

There isn't a company in the world that you can't find fifty things wrong with, if you look. But does it help to look? If we only tell customers about the bad things, aren't we just doing our competitors' job for them? Of course, it's easy to blame 'them' – you don't even have to specify who 'they' are – but if you do that, you show the customer that not only does your company make equipment that breaks down, it can't keep the loyalty of its staff either.

*So you think
you can cope
with customers?*

Don't blame the salesperson

Everyone has examples to tell of bad selling – or at least, customers' versions of bad selling. And the salesperson is at a disadvantage – everyone knows it's his job to sell things, so he's not believed in the same way as a service engineer. After all, he can put the fault right, and the customer is inclined to believe what he says, so his capacity for damage is profound. But if the salesman hadn't sold the machine, where would the service engineer earn his living?

must be the fourth or fifth time this week already. Still haven't got any? Well, how's that then? Yeah, well I mean, how do you expect me to fix these cars? No, well, that's it, isn't it, you don't expect me to fix them, do you? The takeover – what's that got to do with it? Oh, I see. Yeah, all right, I'll tell them, but I can't see them being very happy about it. Yeah, yeah, George, I know you're doing your best, all right, leave it with me – as usual. (*He hangs up.*) Well, you know, I'm very sorry, but since the takeover they got much more cost conscious – at least that's what they call it. And if the takeover wasn't bad enough, now they've put in a computer. What with the computer telling you you don't need it and the takeover management, which doesn't know the first thing about it, telling you you can't afford it – well, you know, all I can do is my best. Let's fill this in, then, and see what happens. Huh, this pen doesn't work – that's typical, it's a company pen!

But Charlie hasn't finished yet. He's still got one more target to deflect the attack on to – the salesman.

Mrs Higgs: Is it difficult?
Charlie: No, it won't take long, the only thing is that you want to clean the brushes on this every time you use it with this carpet.
Mrs Higgs: The last man who repaired it said every three or four times.

Charlie: Yes, you can tell some joker's been at it already.

Mrs Higgs: The salesman said the same thing.

Charlie: Well, what would he know about it? Oh, he might be thinking about the standard model, yeah.

Mrs Higgs: Ah, no, no, no. That was the one I wanted to buy, but he said this one was better for this carpet.

Charlie: Ah, did he? Who was this then?

Mrs Higgs: Mr Harrison.

Charlie: Seen him since?

Mrs Higgs: Yes, he has a stair-cleaner he wants me to buy.

Charlie: When did you buy this?

Mrs Higgs: July.

Charlie: This model went out in May. Did he give you a discount on this? No, he didn't, did he? You'd have got one in the High Street. Yeah, well, I suppose he's got a living to make. Mind you, I could never be a salesman – I'm too truthful. It's me nature, I can't change – no, I could never be a salesman.

Mrs Higgs: They don't actually tell lies, do they?

Charlie: Oh no, not lies, no.

Mrs Higgs: He gave me a guarantee.

Charlie: You didn't sign it, did you?

Mrs Higgs: That'll be him now .
Hello, Mr Harrison, come in.

Mr Harrison: Nice to see you again, Mrs Higgs. (*They shake hands.*)

Charlie: Now count your fingers.

Mr Harrison: Oh, hello, Charlie.
Now, Mrs Higgs, I've brought your stair-cleaner and I think you'll be very happy with it. It's not the one

117

*So you think
you can cope
with customers?*

Give the salesperson an identity

An unnamed salesman is a faceless menace, like a gunman with a stocking mask. But give him an identity, a name, a personality, and make him human, and it's harder to attack him. Calling him by his Christian name is a defence, as is asking for direct evidence of what he tells you.

we were talking about, mind you, but I'm sure it will suit your purposes admirably.

Mrs Higgs: Why?

Mr Harrison: Ah well, I was going to tell you. You would be better with that carpet to have a brush and beat rather than a suck and comb.

Mrs Higgs: Why?

Mr Harrison: Well, it's finer, isn't it?

Charlie: Well, er, bye bye, Mrs Higgs. Be seeing you soon, I expect. Bye bye.

Mrs Higgs: Why do you say that, Mr Harrison? Do you get paid for this? Do you get commission for harrassing lonely women with your bum equipment? All you salesman are liars . . .

Charlie tends to leave a trail of disaster behind him. Still, whatever you say about him, you can't say he has an easy life. No comfy chairs and warm carpeted offices. He works at the sharp end, and half the time he's under the impatient eye of the customer. He works out on his own, the lone ranger, the forgotten man. When he meets a problem, he can't run to the boss's office and ask what to do – he has to find his own way of dealing with it on the spot.

Charlie's life is punctuated by phone calls to the office, and phone boxes that don't work, and switchboard girls who've forgotten him. Half the time they're chewing his ear off because they couldn't get him when they wanted him. The rest of the time, when *he* wants *them*, they don't seem to be there.

So it's little wonder he's the way he is.

I'm putting you on 'hold', Charlie . . .

Charlie works at the sharp end.

*So you think
you can cope
with customers?*

Defend the product

Defend the product by putting it in perspective and measuring it against other products in the price range, not against some unspecified ideal. Put the problem in perspective. No equipment lasts for ever, and the customer may admit that it has done good service in the past. She may even see that other equipment would not have lasted so long. Compare the product to its competition and draw attention to its good points, especially the ones that are unique to it.

But there is another method. You don't have to be a Charlie.

Customer: At last. You don't know what I've been through. I mean, of all times for the equipment to pack up. The last bar of the Sibelius E flat . . . well, can you imagine how I feel?

Service engineer: Indeed I can, sir. What's actually gone wrong?

Customer: What's actually gone wrong? Ha. I fell for a whole lot of smart sales talk. That's what went wrong. Hook, line and sinker. One born every minute. Never again, though. Never again.

Service engineer: That sounds a bit funny, sir. May I ask who it was?

Customer: I don't remember. Tall fellow, fair hair, horn-rimmed spectacles. Serpent's tongue. Scottish accent.

Service engineer: Alastair Mackenzie? Not like him. That really does surprise me. What did Alastair actually tell you?

Customer: Oh, the usual stuff. But I remember one thing he said. He said that this was the best value on the market. Huh!

Service engineer: Yes, well I must say I'd tend to agree with him there. Let's have a look, shall we?

Customer: I suppose I was a fool to buy a load of cheap junk like this in the first place. False economy. I should have spent more and got something decent.

Service engineer: You'd have to spend a lot more to do better than this. Beautiful job!

Customer: Then why did it cut out?

Service engineer: How much do you play it?

Customer: Oh, I don't know. About three or four hours a day, I suppose.

Service engineer: How long have you had it?

Customer: Well, I can tell you. It was my twenty-fifth birthday present. Just on nine years.

Service engineer: First breakdown?

Customer: Yes.

Service engineer: In what – thirteen thousand playing hours?

Customer: Yes. Yes, I suppose so.

Service engineer: Here, have a look at this. Insulation's gone. Must have cut absolutely instantaneously.

Customer: Yes. That's right. That's just what it did. Last bar but one . . .

Service engineer: On some sets you'd have got a current leak. Might have got a nasty shock, but you've got this automatic earth circuit break relay. Don't know why all the manufacturers don't fit them. Cost next to nothing – might save a life.

Customer: Good Lord. Automatic earth circuit break relay. Never realised that.

Service engineer: Well, that's fixed it. If you'd just okay the job sheet.

Customer: Yes, certainly. Yes, of course you've been taken over by Universal International since I bought the set, haven't you? Bet that hasn't made your life any easier.

Service engineer: To tell you the truth, I hardly notice the difference. They leave us pretty well alone. You

'Who sold you this, then?

Defend the company

Defend the company by focusing the customer's attention on the smaller group that actually makes or maintains his equipment rather than the faceless multinational giant that spans the globe. A giant monolithic corporation tends to engender fear and distrust. But in practice, even after a takeover, the small teams and factories usually remain intact, and those are the units that matter to the customer.

*So you think
you can cope
with customers?*

Defend the customer

Defend the customer – remember
he doesn't buy the equipment
because of *how* it works, he buys
it to provide him with the results
he wants. You can only make him
uneasy by implying that he ought
to have known how to repair it.
Instead of criticising him for not
being a good mechanic, why not
make him feel good for having
had the taste and judgement to
buy such a good product?

see, we've all been together so long
in our little factory, they reckon we
know the business better than they
do. Oh, they've given us the new
testing equipment and increased the
staff on quality control. Otherwise,
you wouldn't know there'd been a
takeover.

Customer: I suppose most of your
customers could have fixed this
without dragging you out?

Service engineer: If you'd forgive my
saying so, sir, you're the perfect
customer. We don't make these sets
for radio mechanics, you know. We
make them for music-lovers. You
know, people who can tell the
difference. We always say it's the
educated ear that's our market, not
the itchy screwdriver. If anything
goes wrong, that's what we're here
for. To tell you the truth, the do-it-
yourself gentry can be a bit of a
menace. Oh well, I'll be off now.

On his way out of the room, he trips over
one of the speakers and breaks it.

Service engineer: Terribly sorry. How
absolutely awful of me. I really can't
apologise enough.

Customer: My dear fellow, don't
mention it.

Service engineer: Of course I'll
replace it. The only thing is, I can't
let you have another one before
tomorrow. Let's see, what's the
replacement serial number. Ah . . .
incidentally, what sort of
reproduction has it been giving you?

Customer: Pretty good.

Service engineer: You see, with that quality equipment it would almost be worth investing in a pair of the Superlux Ultratone speakers.

Customer: Superlux Ultratone?

Service engineer: Yes. They really are the ultimate. You can hear the wind section breathing in before their entry.

Customer: No!! Actually breathing in! How fabulous.

Service engineer: I'll have them round this afternoon, then. Hundred and eighty the pair. But of course we'll knock something off because of that.

Customer: No, my dear fellow, don't mention it. Goodness, no . . . complete accident. My fault for leaving it there. Wouldn't hear of it.

Service engineer: Well, you're too kind, sir. I don't deserve it. Many thanks. Let's hope we meet again before I retire.

Customer: I certainly hope so. Bye.

Keep cheerful

Try to make a light-hearted parting remark. 'See you soon,' is not the best parting remark to make when you've just finished servicing the equipment! The customer hopes he won't need to see you again for a long time. The service engineer may be the poor guy who cleans up the mess, but he is also the foundation on which future sales are built.

Defend the company.

Defend the product – put it in
perspective with the competition.

Defend the customer – don't suggest
the equipment has failed because of
what he's done to it.

Defend the company – focus the
customer's attention on a small unit.

Defend the salesperson who sold the
equipment.

Golden rules

9 Welcome, customer

If you work in a shop, it's pretty obvious that you are there to sell to customers. But there are other situations, where your own role may not be defined as sales, but where you could be selling your company's products or services if you put a little thought and effort into it.

Take the International Hotel Group. The staff should act as ambassadors for the hotel, encouraging guests to return by giving good service, and encouraging them to buy all the hotel's facilities. Instead, although 'Welcome' is plastered all over the premises, it's got staff who make guests feel about as welcome as a corpse in a swimming pool.

Mr Knott is in his room, reading from the brochure while he waits for the switchboard to answer. 'Welcome to the International Hotel Group, whose name is synonymous with comfort and courtesy to thousands of satisfied guests here and abroad. Your care is our care. Welcome.'

Telephonist: Hello?

Mr Knott: Oh hello. Thank you for keeping me waiting while you paint your nails and discuss your boyfriends with your fellow telephonists.

Telephonist: Hello?

Mr Knott: Hello. This is Mr Knott of room 704. My bedside lamp doesn't work, the bulb's gone.

Telephonist: Are you sure?

Mr Knott: Sorry? What? Am I sure? No, no, no – I haven't even tried it, it's just a wild guess. I often ring switchboards and tell them my lightbulb's gone.

Welcome, customer.

*So you think
you can cope
with customers?*

Telephonist: Sometimes there's a
loose connection and when the
maintenance man arrives it works
perfectly.

Mr Knott: Well, this one doesn't work
perfectly.

Telephonist: I expect the bulb's gone.

Mr Knott: I just said that.

Telephonist: Which bulb is it?

Mr Knott: I just told you, the bedside
lamp.

Telephonist: I'll put you through to
Maintenance.

Mr Knott: You'll do nothing of the
sort. What's the point of my telling it
all to you if I've got to tell it all over
again. No, no, no – you ring
Maintenance. Oh, and you can ring
Wastepaper Baskets while you're at
it and tell them that my wastepaper
basket may be very elegant and
delightful, but unfortunately it's not
in the room.

The result of that conversation is one
unhappy guest. The switchboard girl
shouldn't have asked him if he was sure
about the lamp. One must never doubt
the customer's word. She didn't listen to
what he said – and if she was going to
put him through to Maintenance, she
should have done it straight away.

Let's try that again, as it should be.

Telephonist: Hello?

Mr Knott: Oh, hello. This is Mr
Knott of room 704, my bedside bulb
doesn't work.

Telephonist: Thank you for telling me,
Mr Knott, I'll send a maintenance
man around as soon as I can.

What could be simpler? She was prompt, she listened, she called him by name, she thanked him, and she notified Maintenance herself.

The switchboard operators are very important. They never meet the guests, but half their contacts in hotels may be on the phone. They have an important part to play in selling the hotel. Everyone is a salesman, even the doorman. He's the first person the guest sees. He should sell him the idea that he is welcome to the hotel and that he is going to enjoy his visit.

It should be like that at the reception desk, too, but Mr Knott wasn't made to feel welcome. He was made to feel like an intruder, like an uninvited guest. That's terrible – a lot of people feel they're stepping into foreign territory when they enter a hotel. They need reassurance, so the first rule must be to make the customer feel at home. All that's needed is:

Clerk: Good evening, sir.
Mr Knott: Evening.
Clerk: If you'll just fill in this form I'll be with you in a moment.

It's easy to do it right, but what happened to Mr Knott?

Clerk: Do you have a reservation, sir?
Mr Knott: Yes I do.
Clerk: Name?
Mr Knott: Knott.
Clerk: Was it our rail-and-room-inclusive package?
Mr Knott: No it wasn't. I didn't know

Be tolerant of awkward customers

Don't take personal offence when a customer is awkward. Try to mend his mood with a brief apology, then get on with your job. If you do it well, and add a little flattery, you may put the customer in a more expansive mood where he'll be receptive to buying more.

*So you think
you can cope
with customers?*

you had a rail-and-room-inclusive
package.

Clerk: Oh yes, 20 per cent reduction.
Well worth it.

Mr Knott: Well, I'll have that then,
thank you.

Clerk: You have to book it before the
commencement of your journey, sir.

Mr Knott: Well, your reservation clerk
didn't tell me that. He could, I
suppose, have assumed that like him
I'm an expert in extra-sensory
perception.

Clerk: Typical. Typical. Do you know,
I'm always having to cover up for
mistakes they make in Reservations.
Time and again it happens.

Mr Knott: It's Knott with a K.

Clerk: I see, Knott with an N.

Mr Knott: No, not with an N.

Clerk: I thought you said it was Knott
with a K.

She didn't apologise for keeping him
waiting. She didn't call him by name
even after he told her what it was. She
behaved as if it was his fault he didn't
know about the rail-and-room package,
and then she blamed someone else
further down the line. And then, to make
it all worse, she couldn't find his booking.

Clerk: I can't find it, sir. Are you sure
you're booked in?

Mr Knott: Yes.

Clerk: Odd.

Mr Knott: Do you have rooms?

Clerk: That's really odd.

Mr Knott: Do you have any rooms?

Clerk: That isn't the point, is it? The

point is, if you've got a booking we ought to be able to find it.

Mr Knott: Well, can't you find me another room and find the booking later?

Clerk: That isn't the system, sir. Ah . . . here it is. You're booked through Modern Lingerie Limited. You travel in ladies underwear. Yes, well, will you register here, sir. I hope you enjoy your stay. Oh, that's good, isn't it. Do you get it? Stay? Underwear? Er . . . room 704.

Mr Knott: Where is it?

Clerk: You'll find it between room 703 and room 705 on the seventh floor. That's between the sixth and the eighth floors, sir.

So she even seemed to blame the customer for not knowing the hotel's routines and systems. She didn't take the opportunity of selling him one single hotel facility. And as if that wasn't enough, she made him unwelcome by her sarcasm.

Add to that a bellboy who doesn't know or care what entertainment is available and Mr Knott is less than happy when he finally gets to his room. He would have liked some light entertainment that evening, but as it is, he'll have to stay in and read his sales reports. Assuming, of course, that he has a light to read by. Still, he has sent for the maintenance man.

Mr Knott: Who is it?
Maintenance man: Maintenance.
Mr Knott: Come in.
Maintenance man: Lightbulb?

Don't limit your role

It's a mistake to define your own role in the company too closely. If you have any contact whatsoever with customers, you are partly a salesman, whatever your main job may be. Even the maintenance man has his part to play as an ambassador, and he'll find it easier if he learns to think of himself as part of the whole organisation rather than working in a small specialised area.

*So you think
you can cope
with customers?*

Mr Knott: Yes.

Maintenance man: Which one is it?

Mr Knott: The one that doesn't work.

Maintenance man: Oh. Right. Oh, they're useless these. Polish. Cutting corners again. They won't learn. They never listen, you know, they seem to think we enjoy replacing these things.

Mr Knott: Don't you like working in this hotel?

Maintenance man: Well, doesn't make any difference to me, does it? I mean, I'm not hotel staff, am I?

Mr Knott: Aren't you?

Maintenance man: I'm Maintenance.

Another missed opportunity to make the guest happy and sell him something. Let's try it again.

Maintenance man: Good evening, sir. Bulb gone in your bedside lamp, is it?

Mr Knott: Ah . . . that's one way of describing the problem.

Maintenance man: Everything else all right, sir? Air-conditioning? Radio? Colour television?

Mr Knott: Oh yes, fine thank you.

Maintenance man: Ah . . . good. There we are, sir. If you do fancy the television, sir, the hotel has a choice of films that you can have plugged to your room. There's a list of titles, sir. All you have to do is telephone down and ask.

Mr Knott: Oh, I may do that. Thank you.

Maintenance man: Have a nice day, sir.

Before he settles down to that reading, Mr Knott has got to eat. Apparently the town isn't exactly an oasis of gastronomic delight, so he decides to go down to the restaurant – where nobody takes any notice of him until he sits down.

Waiter: How many, sir?
Mr Knott: I'm alone.
Waiter: Just one.
Mr Knott: Yes, I think so.
Waiter: That table is reserved, sir.
Mr Knott: Well, it doesn't say reserved on it.
Waiter: No, sir, the headwaiter, he knows that it's reserved, it is marked on his plan.
Mr Knott: What plan?
Waiter: It is in his head. That is our system. You should have waited until you were shown a table.
Mr Knott: When I came in nobody took any notice of me.
Waiter: We are busy, sir.
Mr Knott: So, I sat here.
Waiter: You can't sit there, sir, it is reserved.
Mr Knott: Well, where can I sit?
Waiter: Here, sir.
Mr Knott: What's the difference?
Waiter: It's not reserved.

There is no point in having a system if you don't explain it to the customer. If he knows what the system is he'll co-operate. Moving him on to a different table could make him feel unwelcome, especially if the new table is right next to the kitchen door, with waiters rushing in and out.

The waiter's attitude was all wrong.

There is no point in having a system
if you don't explain it to the customer.

He forgot that the customer was human, and just processed him like a number. And he missed the opportunity to take a drinks order.

Let's try again.

Headwaiter: Good evening, sir, just one?

Mr Knott: Good evening, that's right, yes.

Headwaiter: Are you staying in the hotel?

Mr Knott: Yes I am. Room 704.

Headwaiter: Ah, thank you very much, sir, if you'd come this way.

Mr Knott: Oh, may I sit here?

Headwaiter: I'm awfully sorry, sir . . . if only you'd booked. I'm afraid that table has a reservation. But if you're with us tomorrow night, sir, I'll make sure that that table is reserved for you. Meantime, try this one, and if you're not happy with it, I'll move you to another table as soon as it becomes available. Ehm . . . room 704, Mr Knott. Something to drink, Mr Knott?

That was much better. And even though the customer knew the headwaiter had had to look up his name, it was nice that he took the trouble.

But then Mr Knott had to wait seven and a half minutes for a menu and nearly thirteen minutes to give his order. He could almost feel his clothes going out of fashion.

Waiter: Are you ready to order, sir?

Mr Knott: H'mm. It rarely takes me more than twenty-three minutes, I'll

*So you think
you can cope
with customers?*

have the chef's pâté. And is there
anything in particular that you'd
recommend?

Waiter: Everything, sir.

Mr Knott: Oh, that's good. That's
very helpful. That narrows it down a
bit. Well, I fancy fish. What exactly
is the chef's speciality – the *goujons
de poisson à la marseillaise?*

Waiter: Eh . . . isa bits of fish, sir, in
a . . . in a special sauce.

Mr Knott: How informative. I won't
have that.

Waiter: We have lobster, sir. It's
very . . .

Mr Knott: Expensive, yes it is.

Waiter: Eh . . . the crayfish.

Mr Knott: Even more expensive. I'm
not likely to have that if I think the
lobster is too expensive. No, I'll have
the grilled mackerel.

Waiter: The mackerel is finished, sir.

Mr Knott: You couldn't have told me
that when you handed me the menu,
of course?

Waiter: No, sir, it wasn't finished
then.

Mr Knott: No, of course not. That
was half an hour ago. In the
meantime, I've sat here growing
older and watching all the mackerel
being ordered.

Waiter: How about . . . a nice fillet
steak, sir?

Mr Knott: What a very sensible
suggestion. I don't want anything
expensive. I do want fish. I can't
have the grilled mackerel, so you
offer me the fillet steak as nearest.
All right. I *will* have a tomato
omelette.

The waiter didn't fetch the wine waiter. By the time he arrived it was too late, so Mr Knott didn't order any wine, which he would have liked (and on which there is a good mark-up). Still, at least the waiter tried to sell him the most expensive things on the menu. But that isn't always the most tactful thing to do with an awkward customer. He'll leave the restaurant in a bolshy mood, and it probably won't have worn off in the morning when he goes to check out.

Mr Knott: Knott. Room 704.
Cashier: Right, sir.
Mr Knott: Thank you. What's this?
   T £1.65?
Cashier: Yes, sir.
Mr Knott: I didn't have any tea. And even if I did, I wouldn't have had £1.65's worth.
Cashier: T is for telephone.
Mr Knott: Oh . . . yes, yes I did make a couple of calls. What's this?
   D £7.80.
Cashier: Dinner, sir. The symbols are on the back.
Mr Knott: £7.80 for dinner?
Cashier: Well, it is inclusive.
Mr Knott: Inclusive of what?
Cashier: Ehm . . . food.
Mr Knott: Well, of course it's inclusive of food. £7.80 for a tomato omelette?
Cashier: Eh . . . drinks.
Mr Knott: Didn't have any.
Cashier: No drinks, sir?
Mr Knott: No drinks. What's this?
   W £4.60? Women? Water?
Cashier: Wine, sir.
Mr Knott: Well, a) I didn't have any,

Don't oversell

Overselling can act against your own interests, as it tends to annoy the customer if you persist. What you want is a happy customer, because a happy customer will want to return and recommend others to come. If a customer makes it clear that he doesn't want an expensive item, you should accept it gracefully. A good rule is to avoid conversation where you find yourself saying, 'Ah, but . . .'

If a customer makes it clear he doesn't want an expensive item you should accept it gracefully.

and b) you just said it was inclusive.

Cashier: I have the waiter's check here.

Man behind: Look, do you think you could hurry up. I've got a train to catch.

Mr Knott: What's this? Bolster soup?

Cashier: Lobster soup.

Mr Knott: I had chef's pâté.

Cashier: Well, it could be chef's pâté. I'll have to see the Duty Manager, sir.

The cashier should have called for the Duty Manager as soon as she realised Mr Knott was going to query his bill, instead of keeping everyone else waiting. Even if she was under pressure, she should have been polite. Let's give her another try.

Mr Knott: What's this? T £1.65?

Cashier: Oh, that's the telephone, Mr Knott. The symbols are on the back of the bill. It's difficult to make them clear, so if there are any others you don't understand, do ask.

Mr Knott: Yes, D £7.80. W £4.60?

Cashier: Dinner £7.80, and wine £4.60.

Mr Knott: Ah yes. Oh . . . I didn't have any wine.

Cashier: Didn't you? Oh I'm very sorry about that, would you excuse me a moment? Mr Williams?

Duty Manager: You have a query, sir?

Mr Knott: Yes, indeed I have.

Duty Manager: Well, let's see if I can sort it out for you, shall we?

Mr Knott: Well, I didn't have any wine, for a start.

*So you think
you can cope
with customers?*

Duty Manager: You didn't have any
   wine?

Mr Knott: And you're charging me
   £7.80 for a tomato omelette.

Duty Manager: Are you in a hurry,
   sir?

Mr Knott: Yes, as a matter of fact I
   am.

Duty Manager: I'll have a porter
   order a taxi for you while I clear this
   up.

Mr Knott: Thank you.

Hassle over the bill can be the final
straw, especially if you compound it by
recreating the Spanish Inquisition over
payment.

Cashier: We don't accept cheques
   without identification. Do you have
   other identification?

He may be leaving, but at least you
could sell him the idea of coming back.

Cashier: Oh, do you have a banker's
   card, Mr Knott?

Mr Knott: Yes, here we are.

Cashier: Thank you, Mr Knott. I do
   hope you had a pleasant stay.

Mr Knott: No, I did *not!!*

Cashier: Oh? That's very unusual.
   You must come and stay with us
   again, we can put that right.

What may seem to you to be a single,
one-night-only customer could be a
company executive looking for somewhere to hold a week's convention for
five hundred delegates. If you don't look
after him properly, another hotel will get

the benefit of that business, instead of your company.

There's no such thing as a captive clientèle

Even in a busy hotel or restaurant where the customers are all transients, it's wrong to assume there will be plenty more to come. The individual you are off-hand with today may never need to come back himself, but don't assume it doesn't matter. If you upset him, he will tell his friends and eventually the word will get around. There's no such thing as a captive clientèle any more — people who have cars (and most do) will think nothing of driving a little further to go somewhere that treats them as they want to be treated.

Golden rules

Make the customer feel welcome and at home by using his name.

Know what your company has to offer and promote its amenities.

If you can't sell him anything else, then make sure you sell him the idea of coming back again.

Summary

It is not always easy to sell goods or services in this highly competitive world. Most of us are not selling unique merchandise or services. Customers can, in a sense, 'go next door' to find another organisation offering similar things. So good customer relations are what persuade a looker and a browser to become a regular customer and make the regular customer stay just that. So customer relations skills are vital if you want to succeed.

It is very simple, really. There are two main things to remember:

- The customer is not a nuisance but an essential part of the job – no customers, no job.
- Treat customers in the same way as you like to be treated yourself.

A Selected List of Non-Fiction Available from Mandarin Books

While every effort is made to keep prices low, it is sometimes necessary to increase prices at short notice. Mandarin Paperbacks reserves the right to show new retail prices on covers which may differ from those previously advertised in the text or elsewhere.

The prices shown below were correct at the time of going to press.

☐	7493 0000 0	**Moonwalk**	Michael Jackson	£3.99
☐	7493 0004 3	**South Africa**	Graham Leach	£3.99
☐	7493 0010 8	**What Fresh Hell is This?**	Marion Meade	£3.99
☐	7493 0011 6	**War Games**	Thomas Allen	£3.99
☐	7493 0013 2	**The Crash**	Mihir Bose	£4.99
☐	7493 0014 0	**The Demon Drink**	Jancis Robinson	£4.99
☐	7493 0015 9	**The Health Scandal**	Vernon Coleman	£4.99
☐	7493 0016 7	**Vietnam – The 10,000 Day War**	Michael Maclear	£3.99
☐	7493 0049 3	**The Spycatcher Trial**	Malcolm Turnbull	£3.99
☐	7493 0022 1	**The Super Saleswoman**	Janet Macdonald	£4.99
☐	7493 0023 X	**What's Wrong With Your Rights?**	Cook/Tate	£4.99
☐	7493 0024 8	**Mary and Richard**	Michael Burn	£3.50
☐	7493 0061 2	**Voyager**	Yeager/Rutan	£3.99
☐	7493 0060 4	**The Fashion Conspiracy**	Nicholas Coleridge	£3.99
☐	7493 0027 2	**Journey Without End**	David Bolton	£3.99
☐	7493 0028 0	**The Common Thread**	Common Thread	£4.99

All these books are available at your bookshop or newsagent, or can be ordered direct from the publisher. Just tick the titles you want and fill in the form below.

Mandarin Paperbacks, Cash Sales Department, PO Box 11, Falmouth, Cornwall TR10 9EN.

Please send cheque or postal order, no currency, for purchase price quoted and allow the following for postage and packing:

UK   55p for the first book, 22p for the second book and 14p for each additional book ordered to a maximum charge of £1.75.

BFPO and Eire   55p for the first book, 22p for the second book and 14p for each of the next seven books, thereafter 8p per book.

Overseas Customers   £1.00 for the first book plus 25p per copy for each additional book.

NAME (Block Letters) ....

ADDRESS ....

....